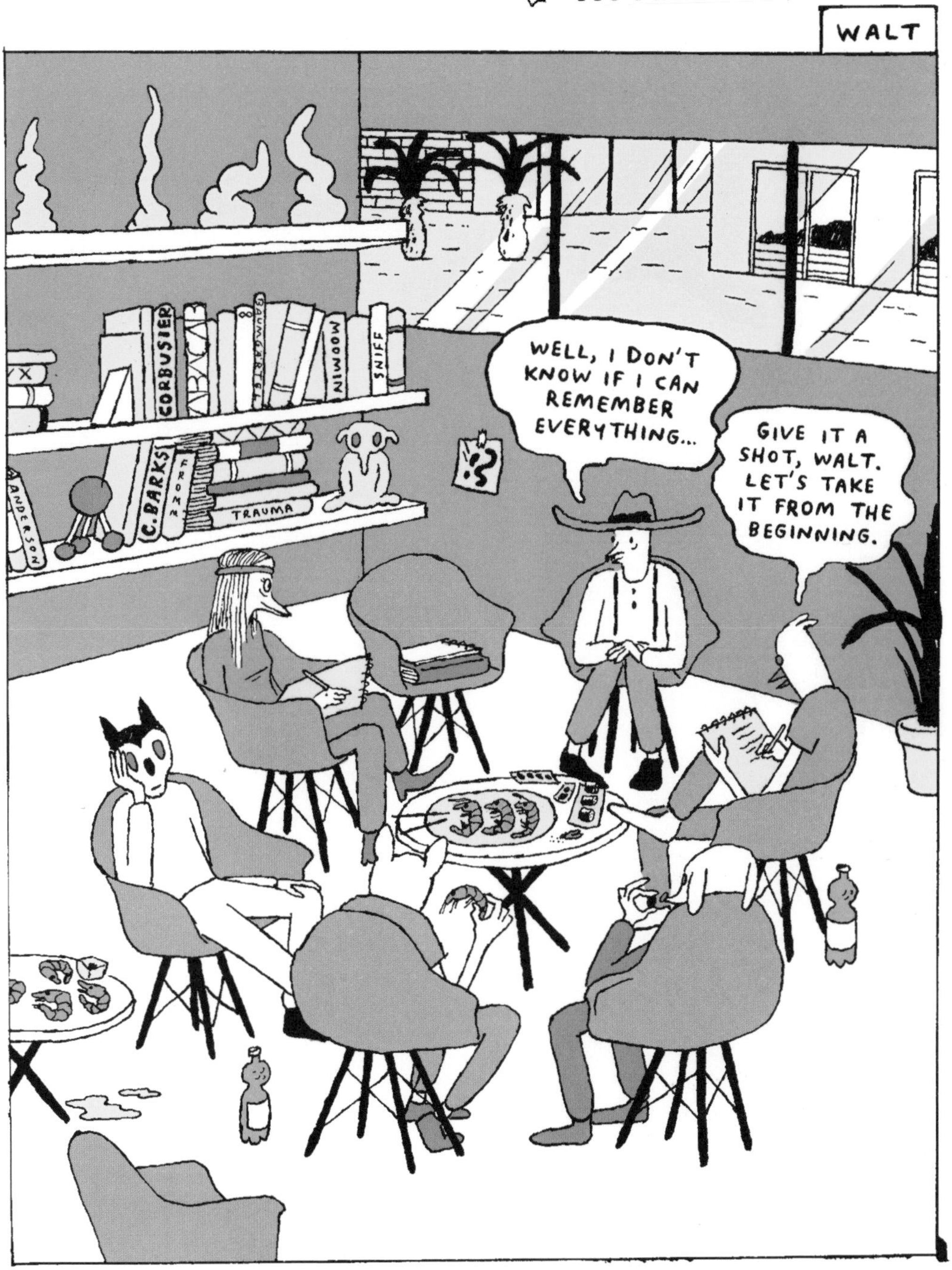
WALT
CORBUSIER
MOOMIN
SNIFF
C.BARKS
FROMM
TRAUMA
ANDERSON
WELL, I DON'T KNOW IF I CAN REMEMBER EVERYTHING...
GIVE IT A SHOT, WALT. LET'S TAKE IT FROM THE BEGINNING.

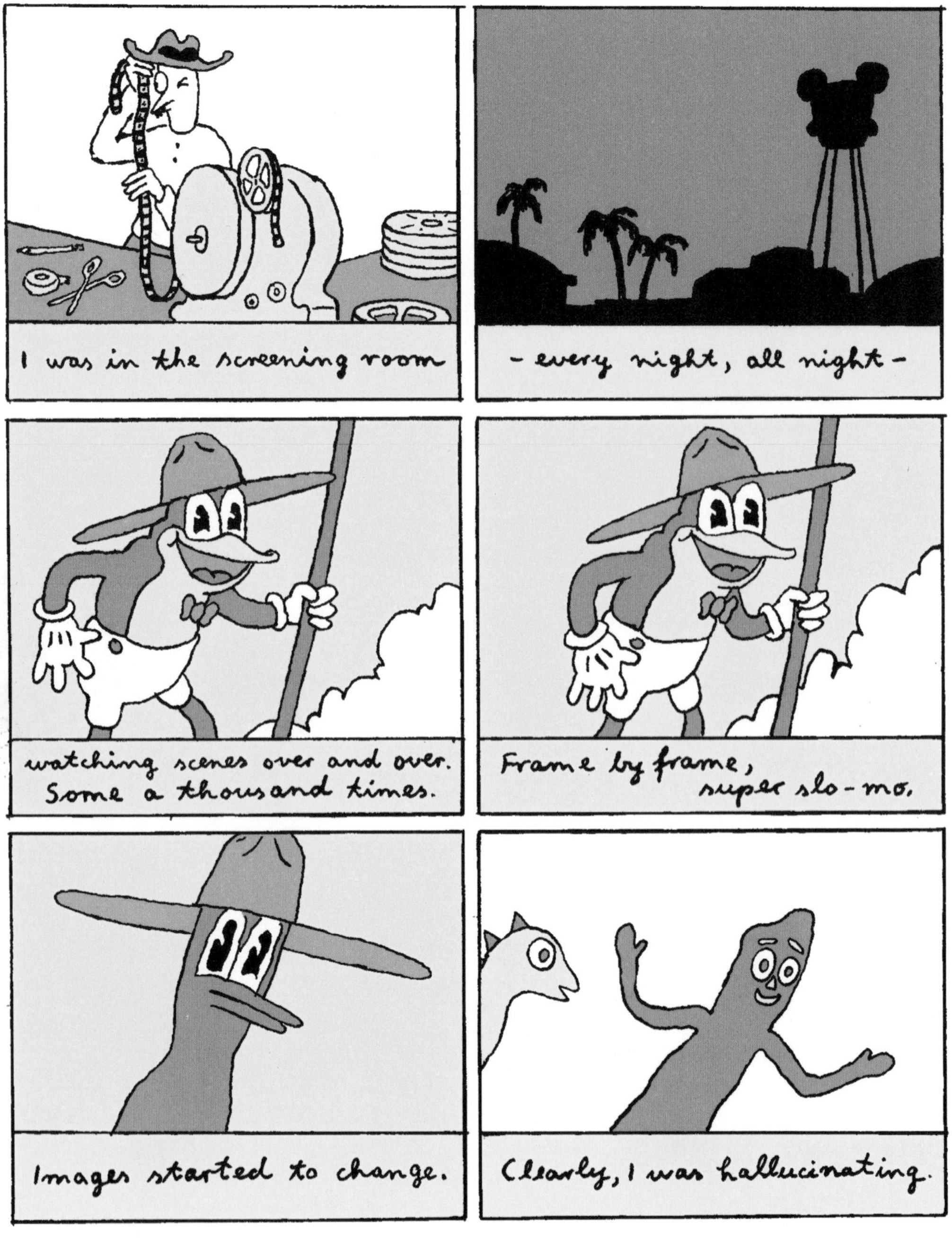
I was in the screening room
- every night, all night -
watching scenes over and over. Some a thousand times.
Frame by frame, super slo-mo.
Images started to change.
Clearly, I was hallucinating.

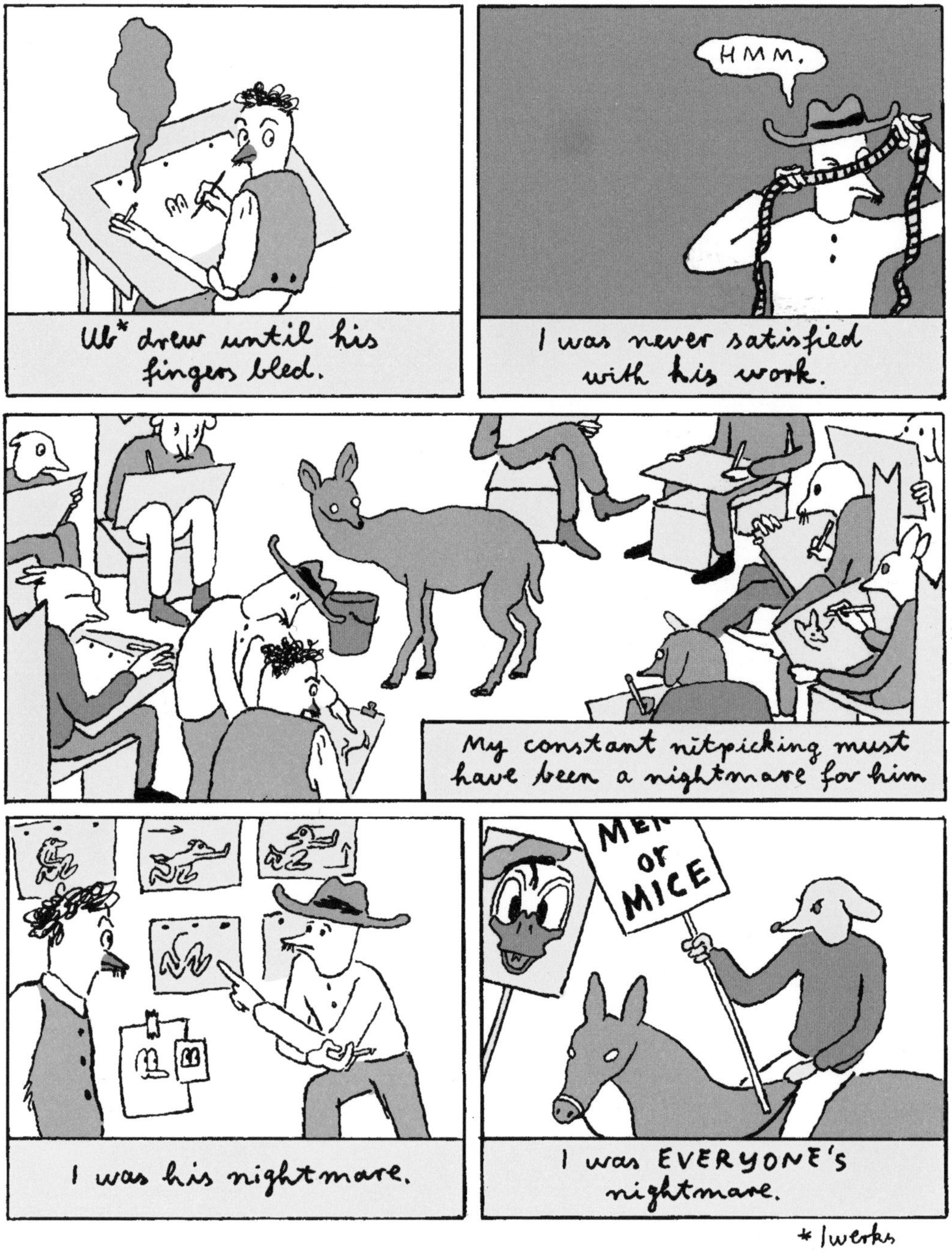
Ub* drew until his fingers bled.
HMM.
I was never satisfied with his work.
My constant nitpicking must have been a nightmare for him
I was his nightmare.
MEN or MICE
I was EVERYONE'S nightmare.
*Iwerks

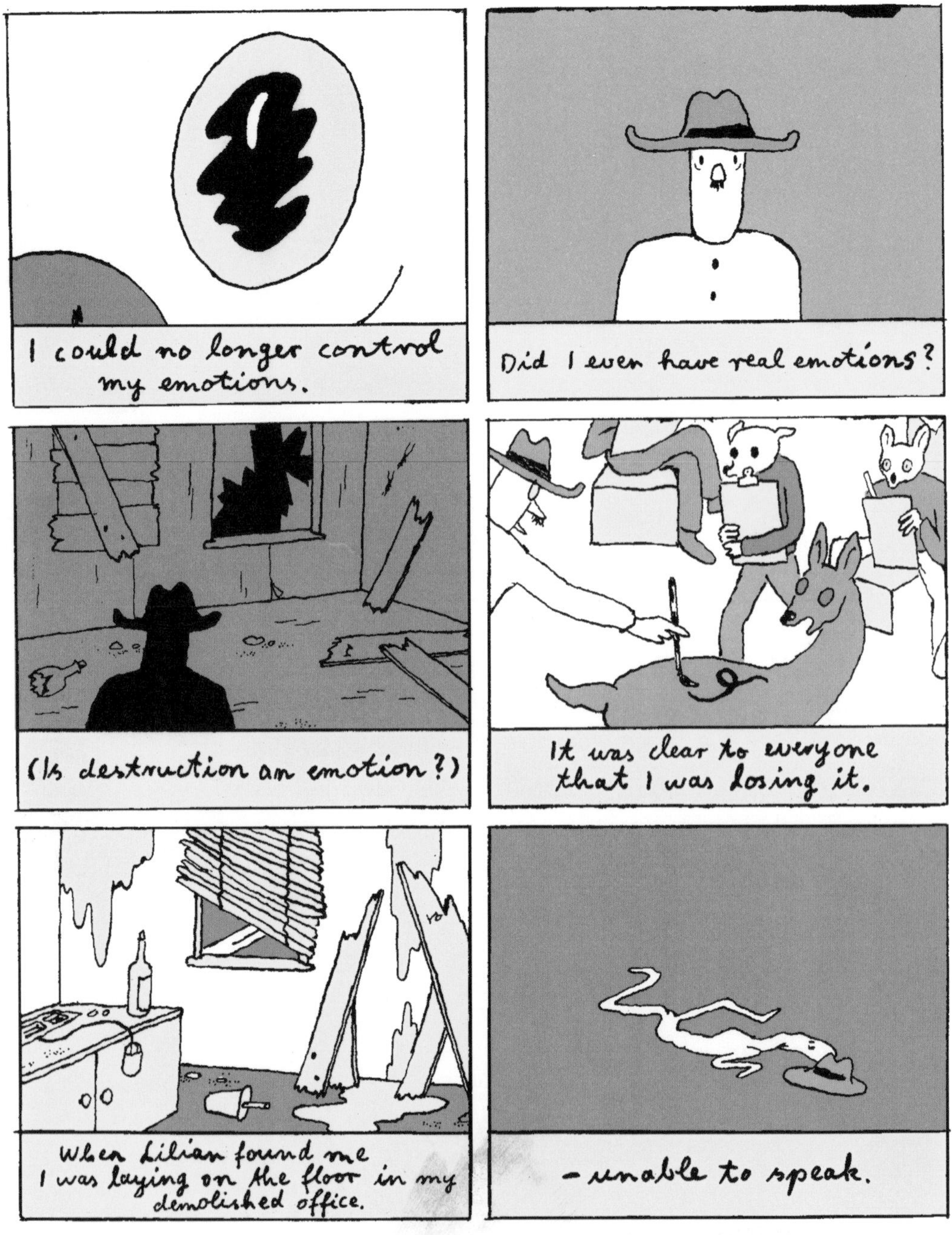
I could no longer control my emotions.
Did I ever have real emotions?
(Is destruction an emotion?)
It was clear to everyone that I was losing it.
When Lilian found me I was laying on the floor in my demolished office.
- unable to speak.

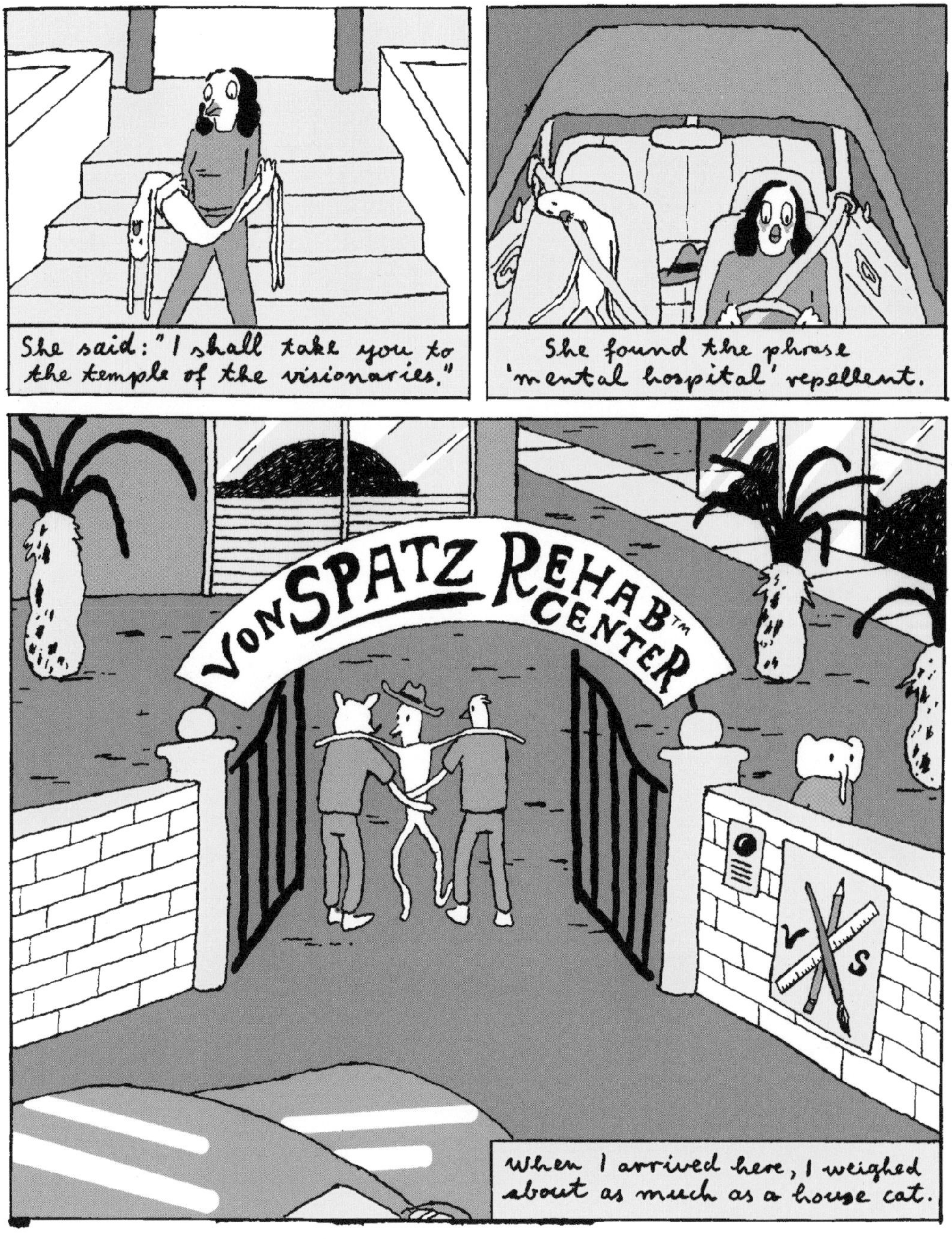
She said: "I shall take you to the temple of the visionaries."
She found the phrase 'mental hospital' repellent.
VON SPATZ REHAB™ CENTER
When I arrived here, I weighed about as much as a house cat.

THE EXERCISE

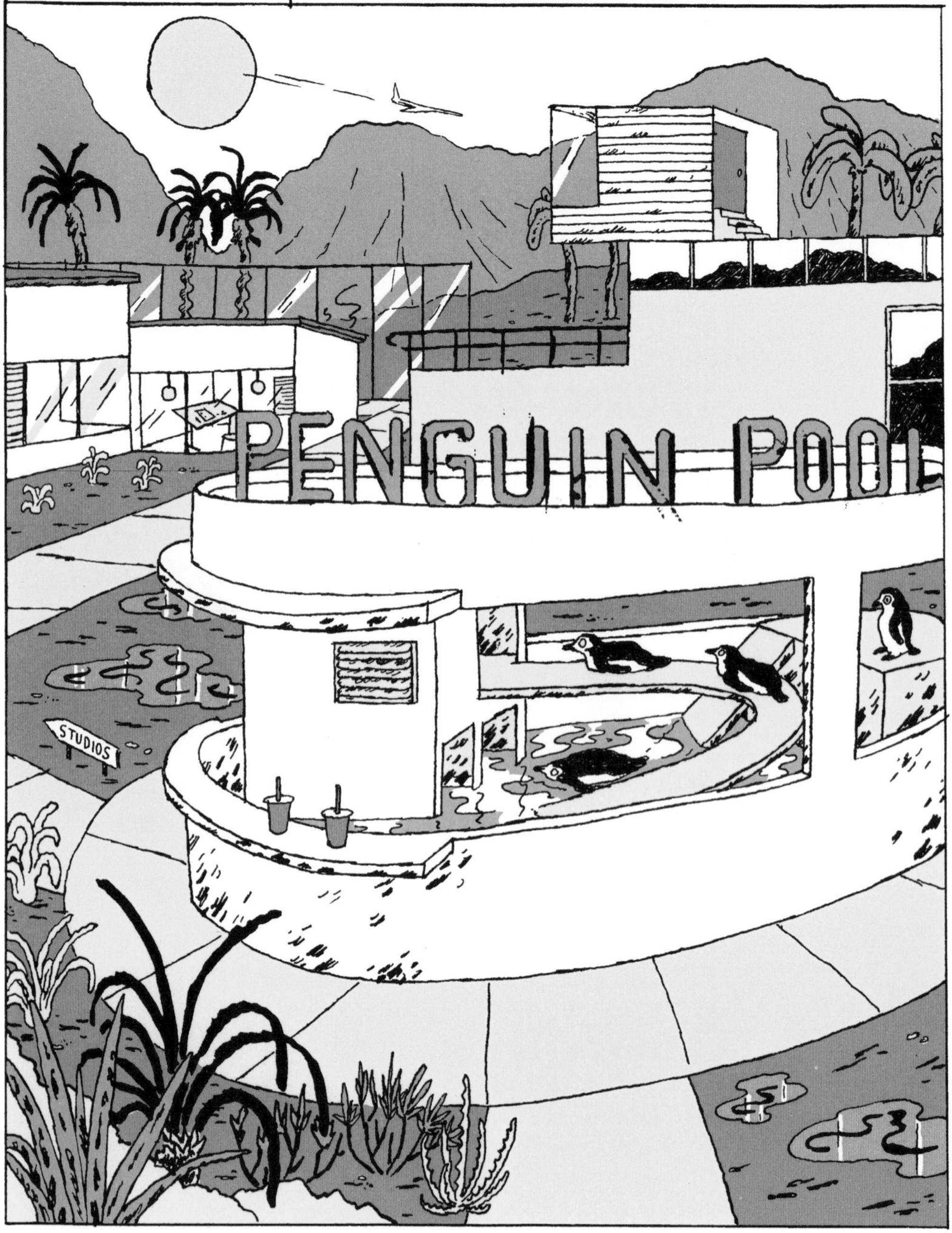

PENGUIN POOL
STUDIOS

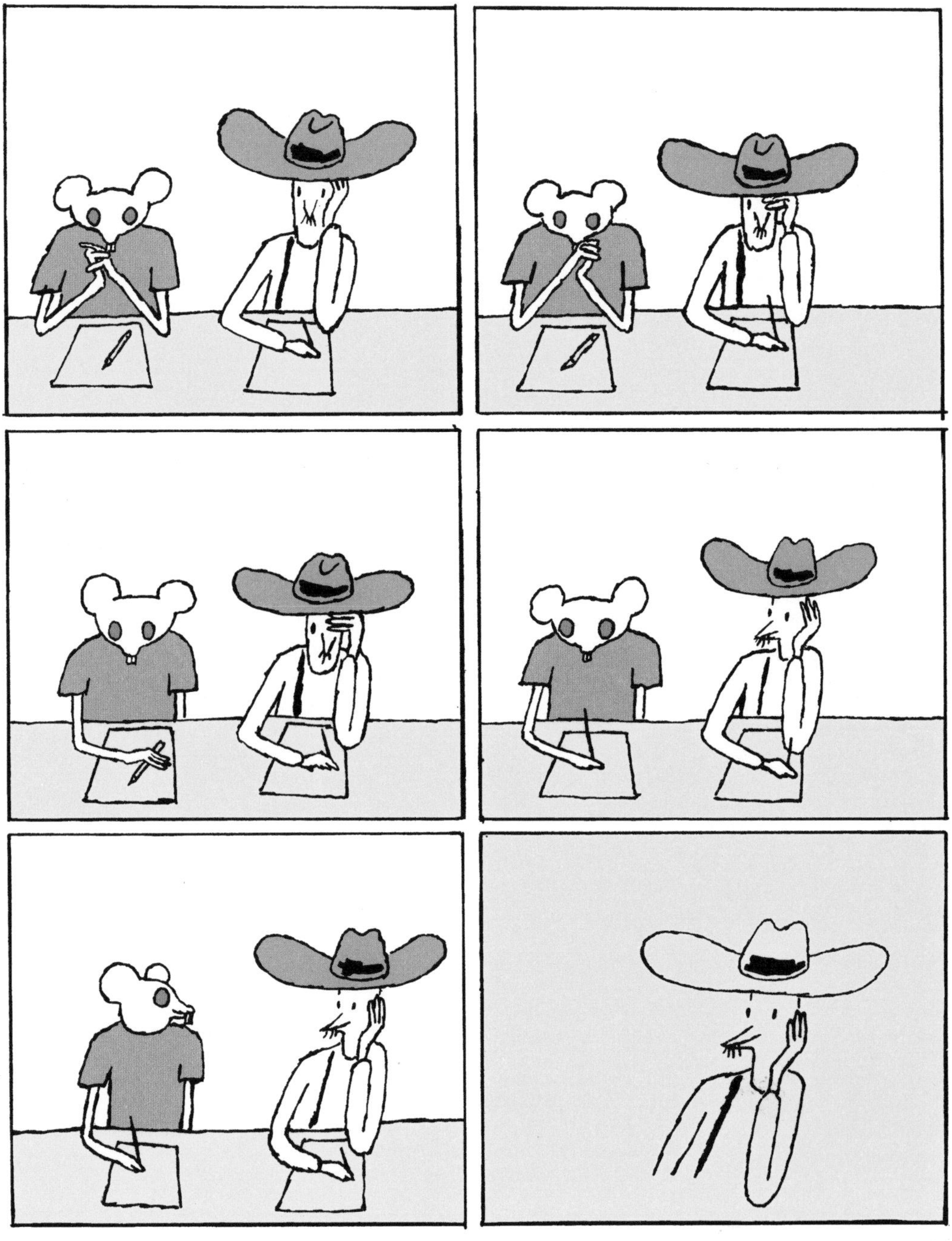

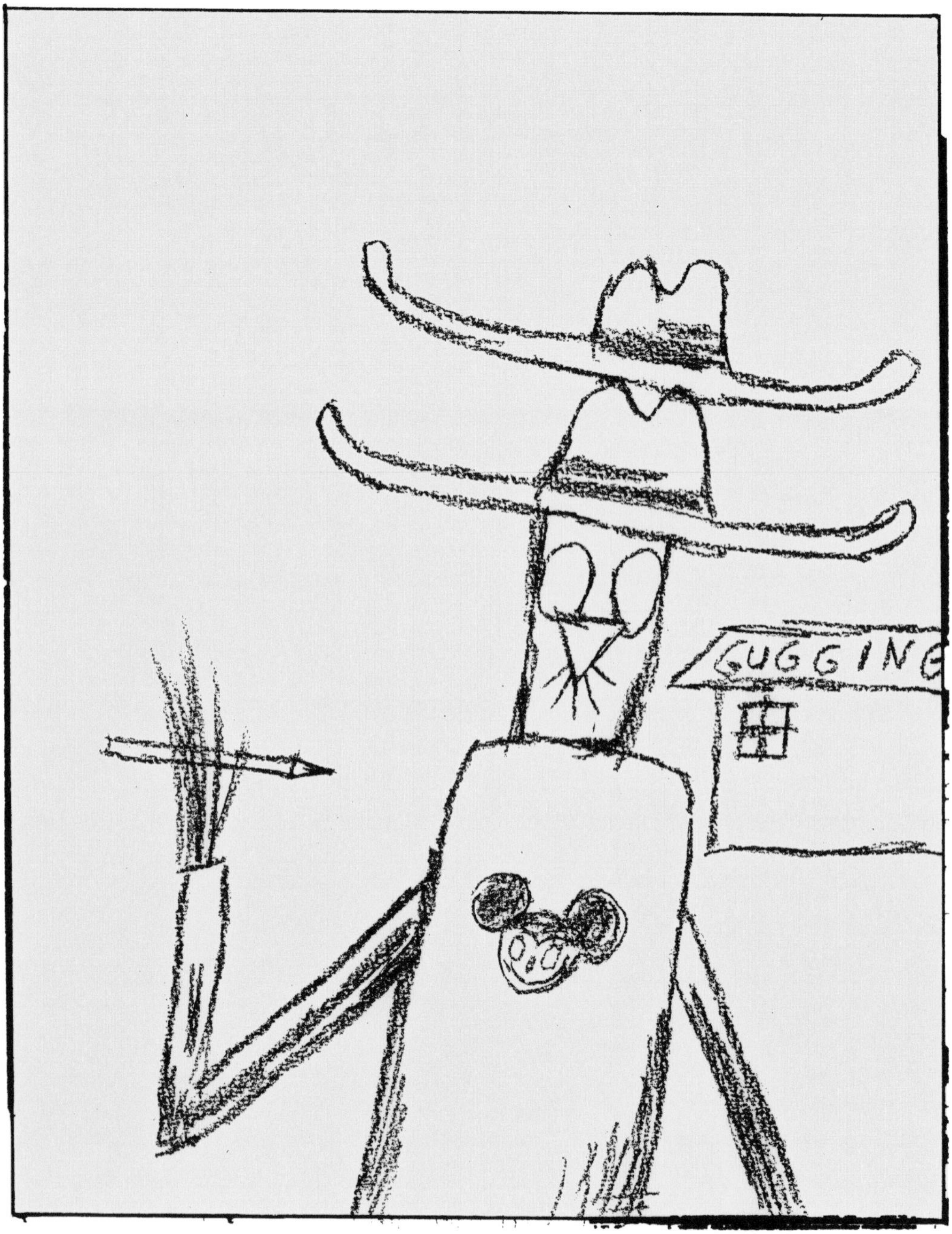
GUGGING

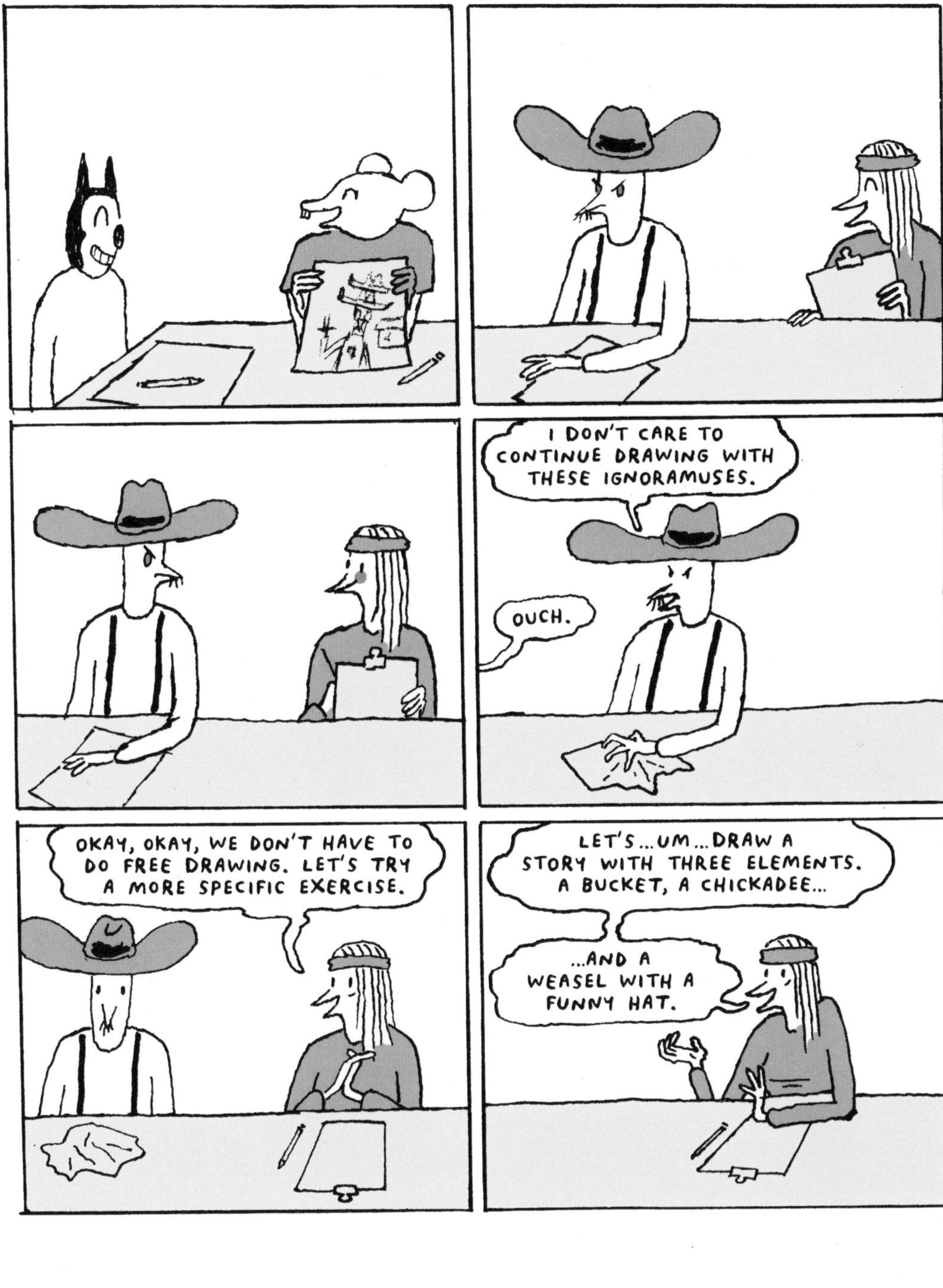
I DON'T CARE TO CONTINUE DRAWING WITH THESE IGNORAMUSES.
OUCH.
OKAY, OKAY, WE DON'T HAVE TO DO FREE DRAWING. LET'S TRY A MORE SPECIFIC EXERCISE.
LET'S...UM...DRAW A STORY WITH THREE ELEMENTS. A BUCKET, A CHICKADEE...
...AND A WEASEL WITH A FUNNY HAT.

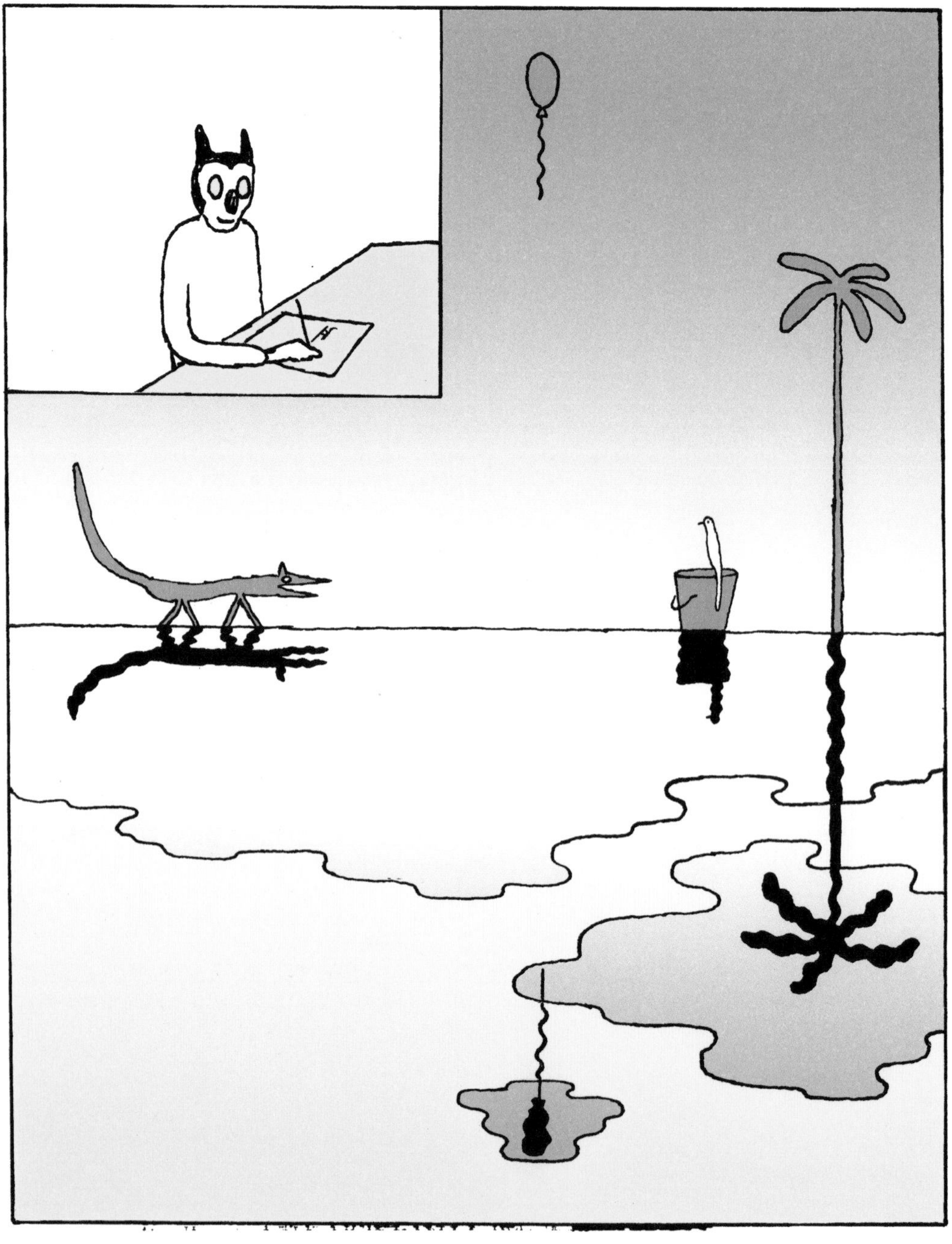

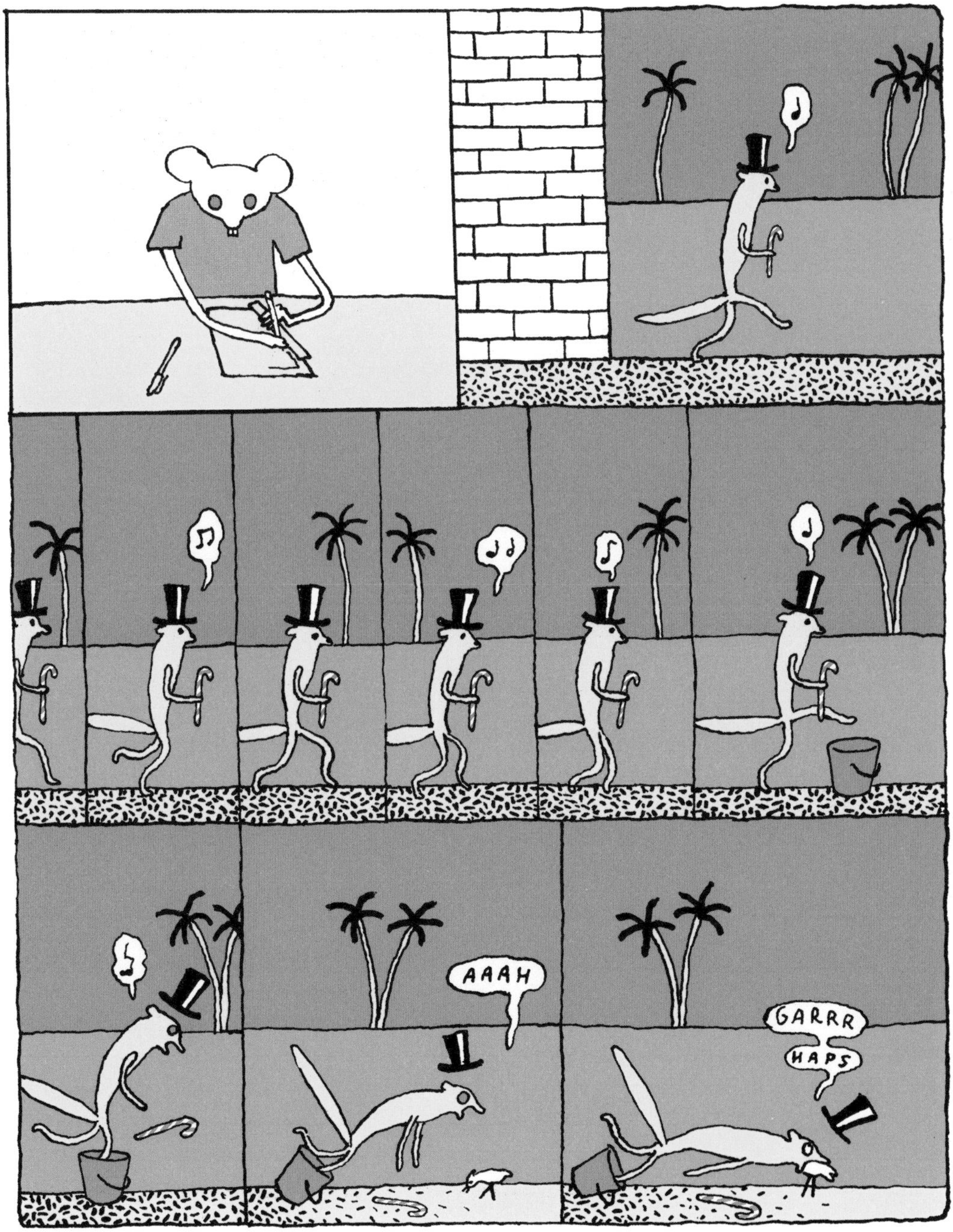
AAAH
GARRR
HAPS

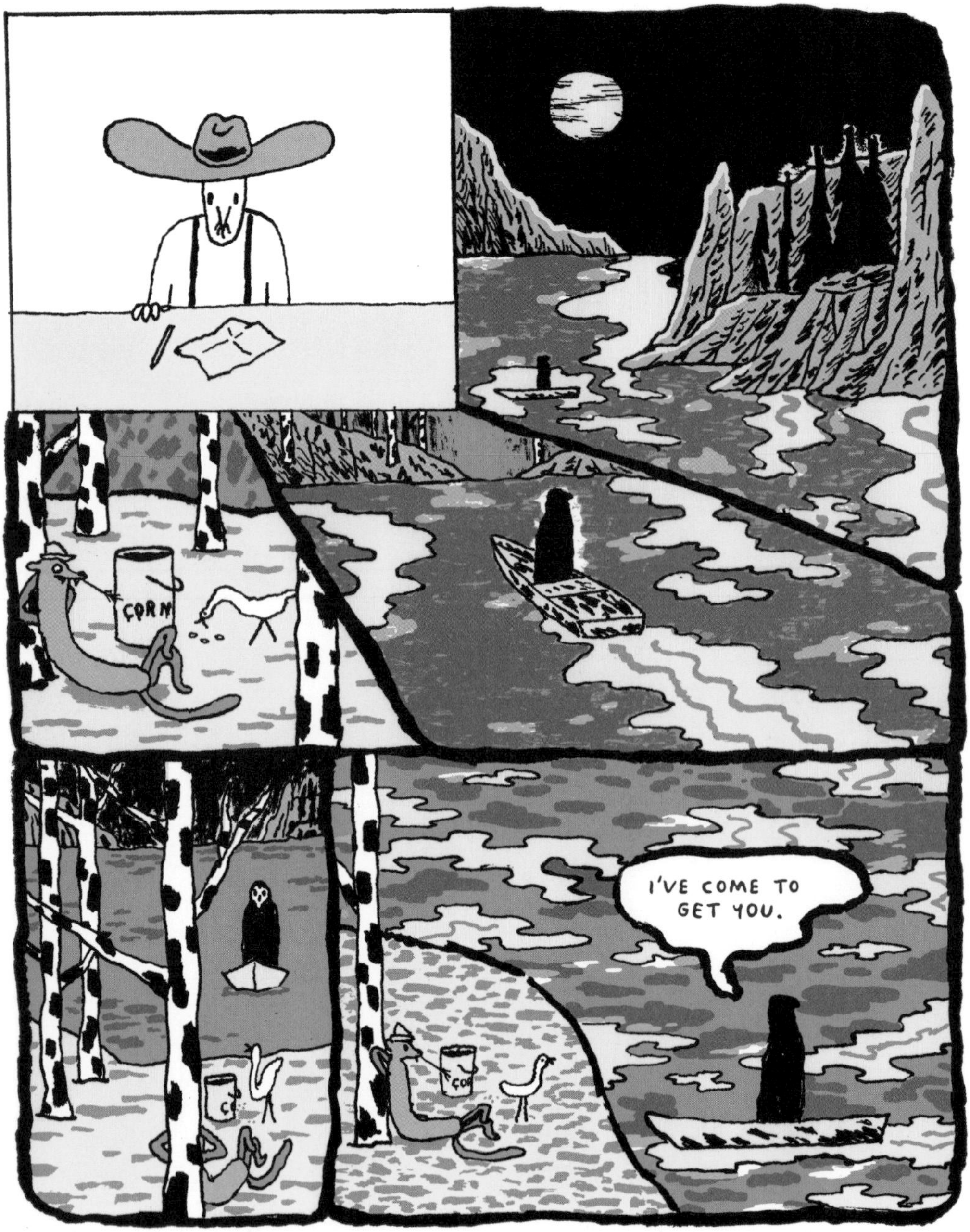
ÇORN
I'VE COME TO GET YOU.

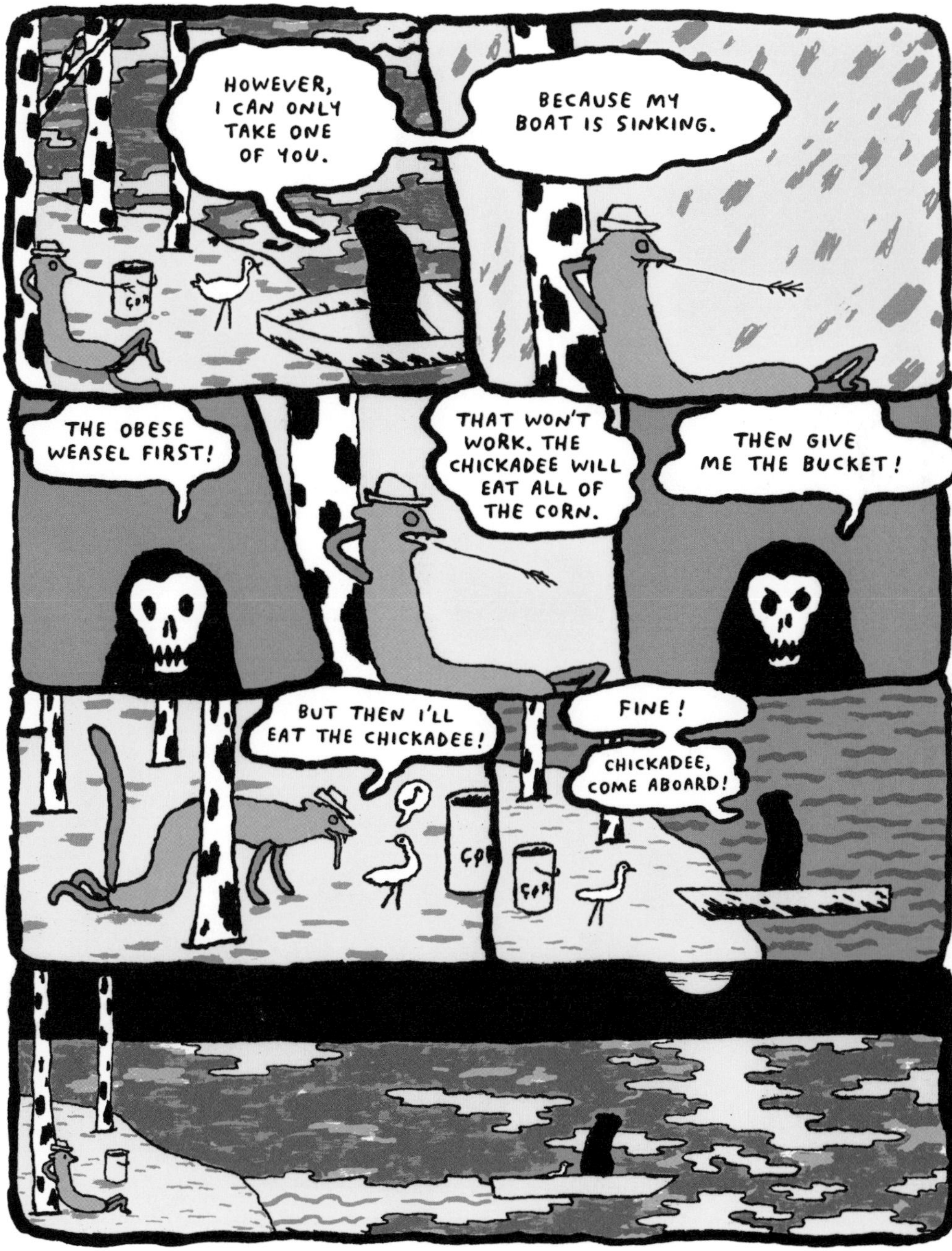
HOWEVER, I CAN ONLY TAKE ONE OF YOU.
BECAUSE MY BOAT IS SINKING.
THE OBESE WEASEL FIRST!
THAT WON'T WORK. THE CHICKADEE WILL EAT ALL OF THE CORN.
THEN GIVE ME THE BUCKET!
BUT THEN I'LL EAT THE CHICKADEE!
FINE!
CHICKADEE, COME ABOARD!

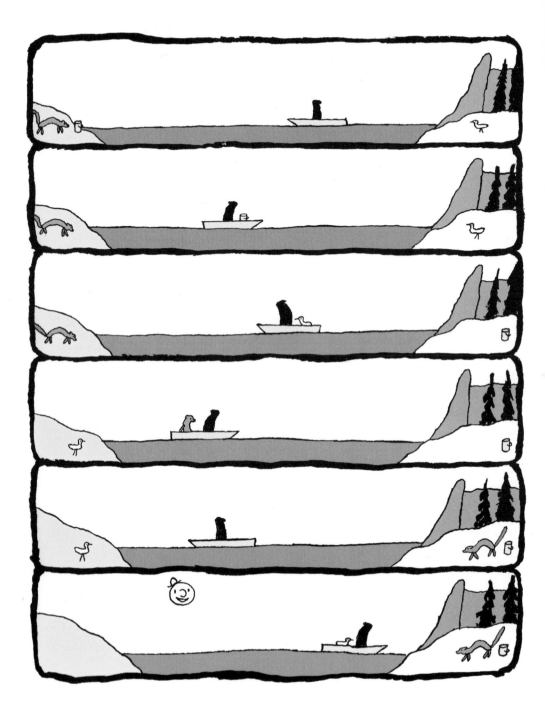

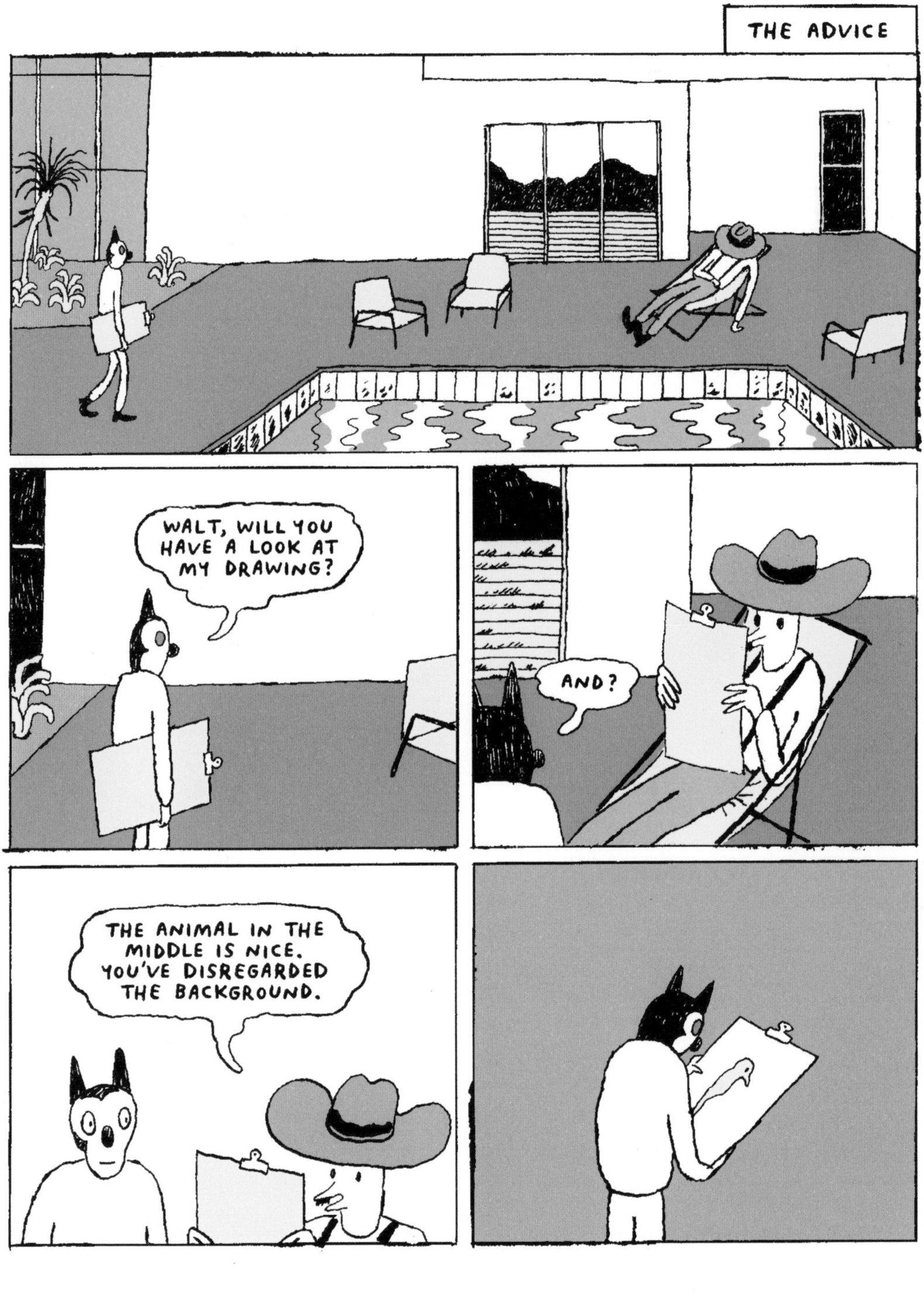
THE ADVICE
WALT, WILL YOU HAVE A LOOK AT MY DRAWING?
AND?
THE ANIMAL IN THE MIDDLE IS NICE. YOU'VE DISREGARDED THE BACKGROUND.

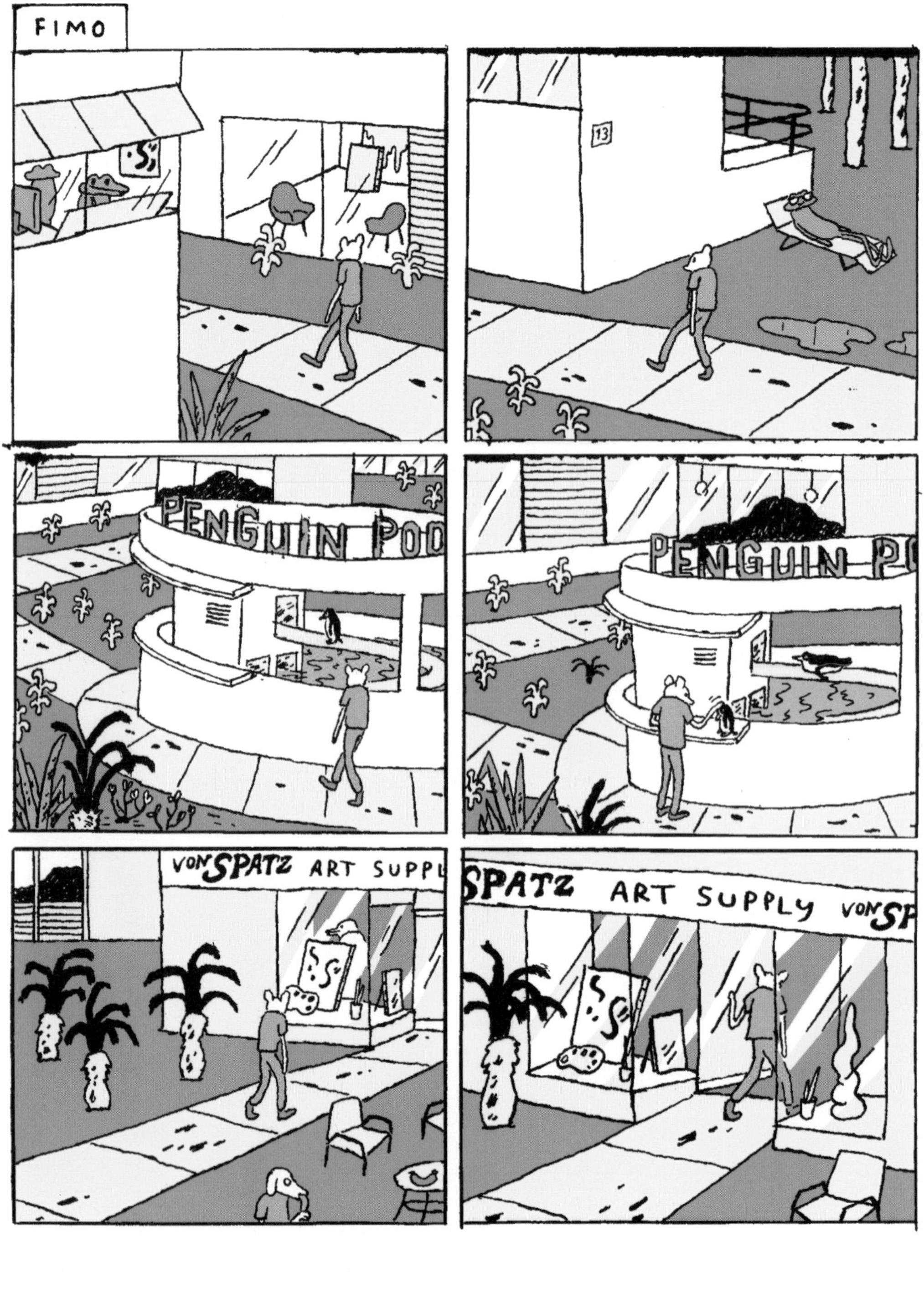
FIMO
13
PENGUIN POO
PENGUIN PO
VON SPATZ ART SUPPL
SPATZ ART SUPPLY VON SP

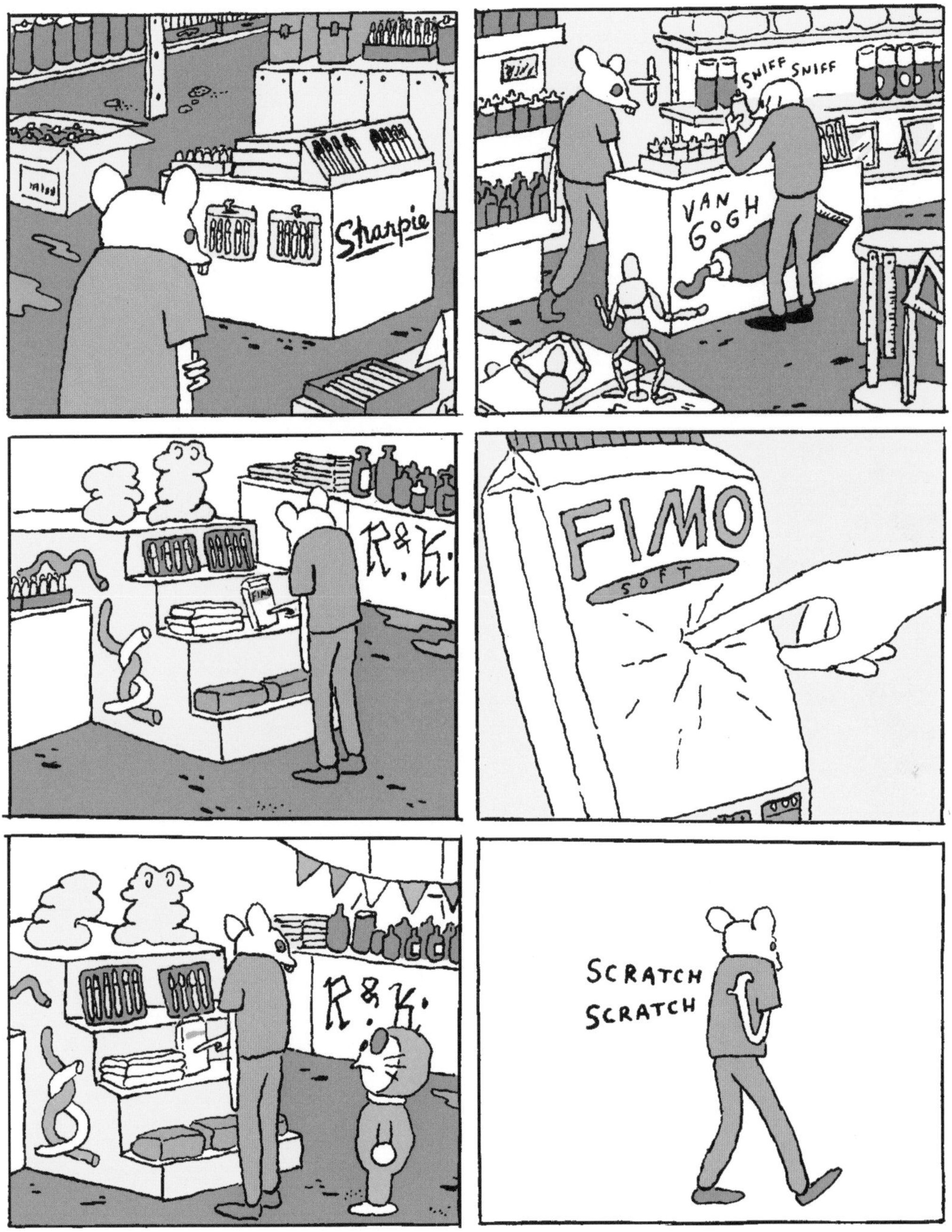
Sharpie
VAN GOGH
SNIFF SNIFF
R & K.
FIMO
SOFT
R & K.
SCRATCH
SCRATCH

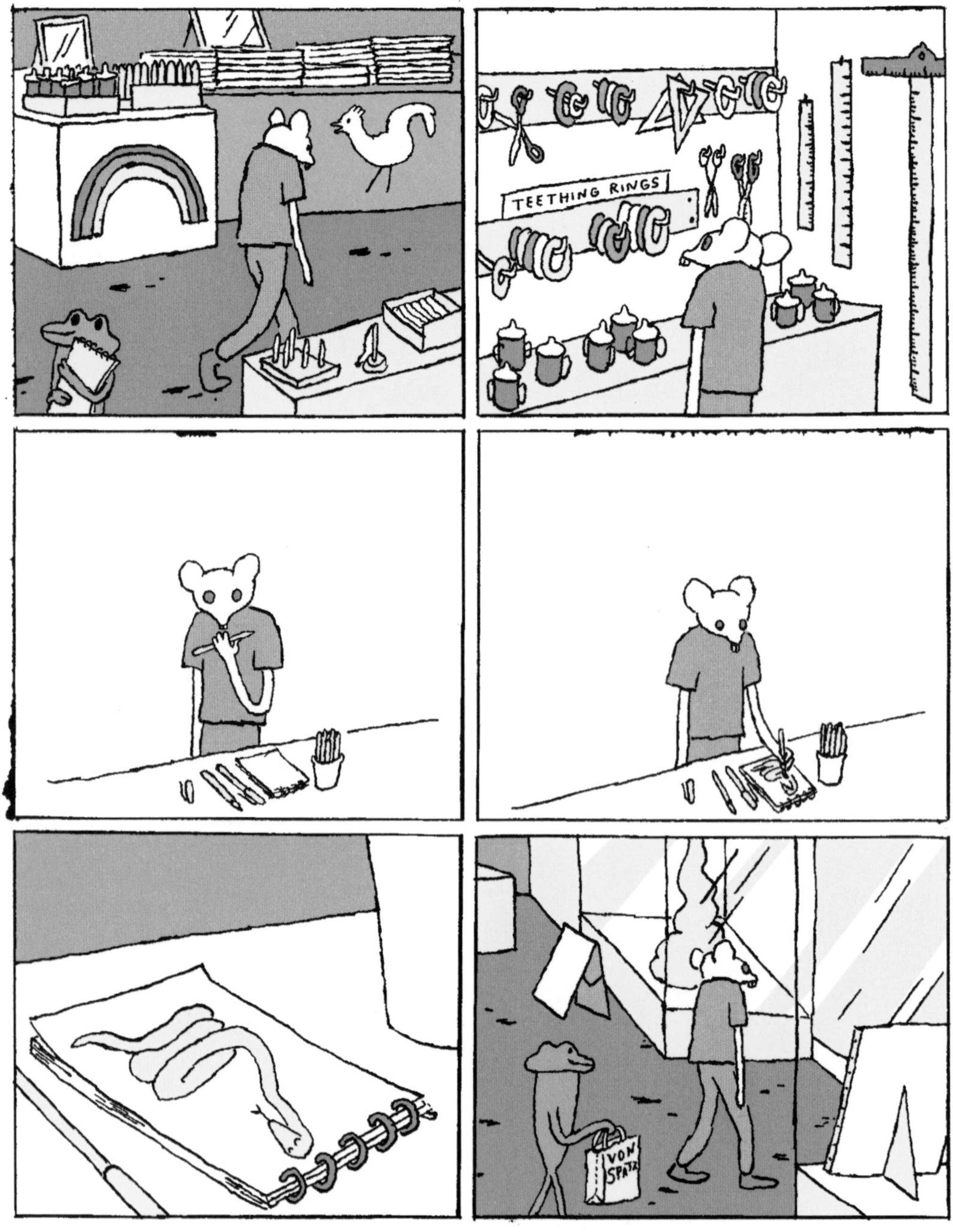
TEETHING RINGS
VON SPATZ

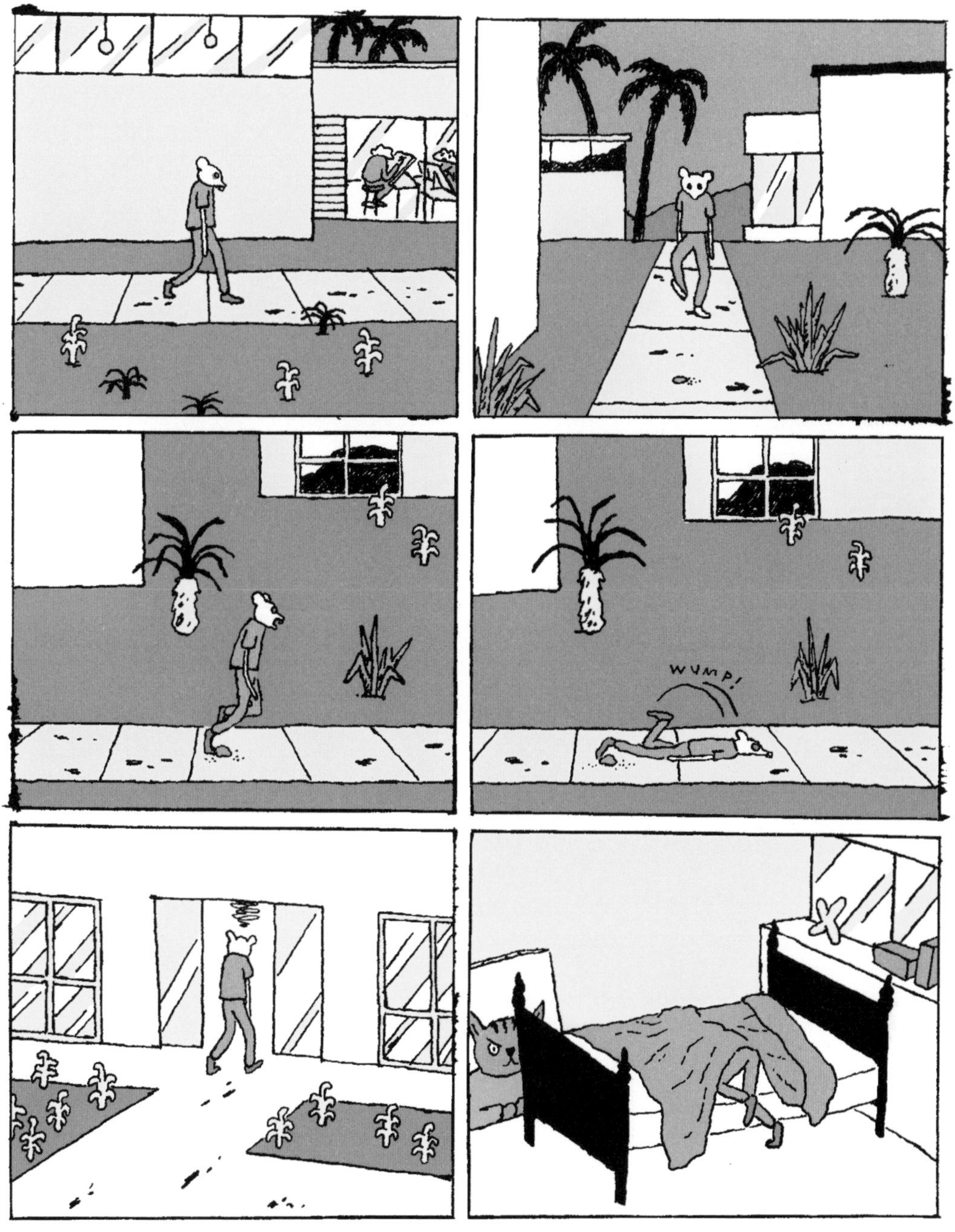
WUMP!

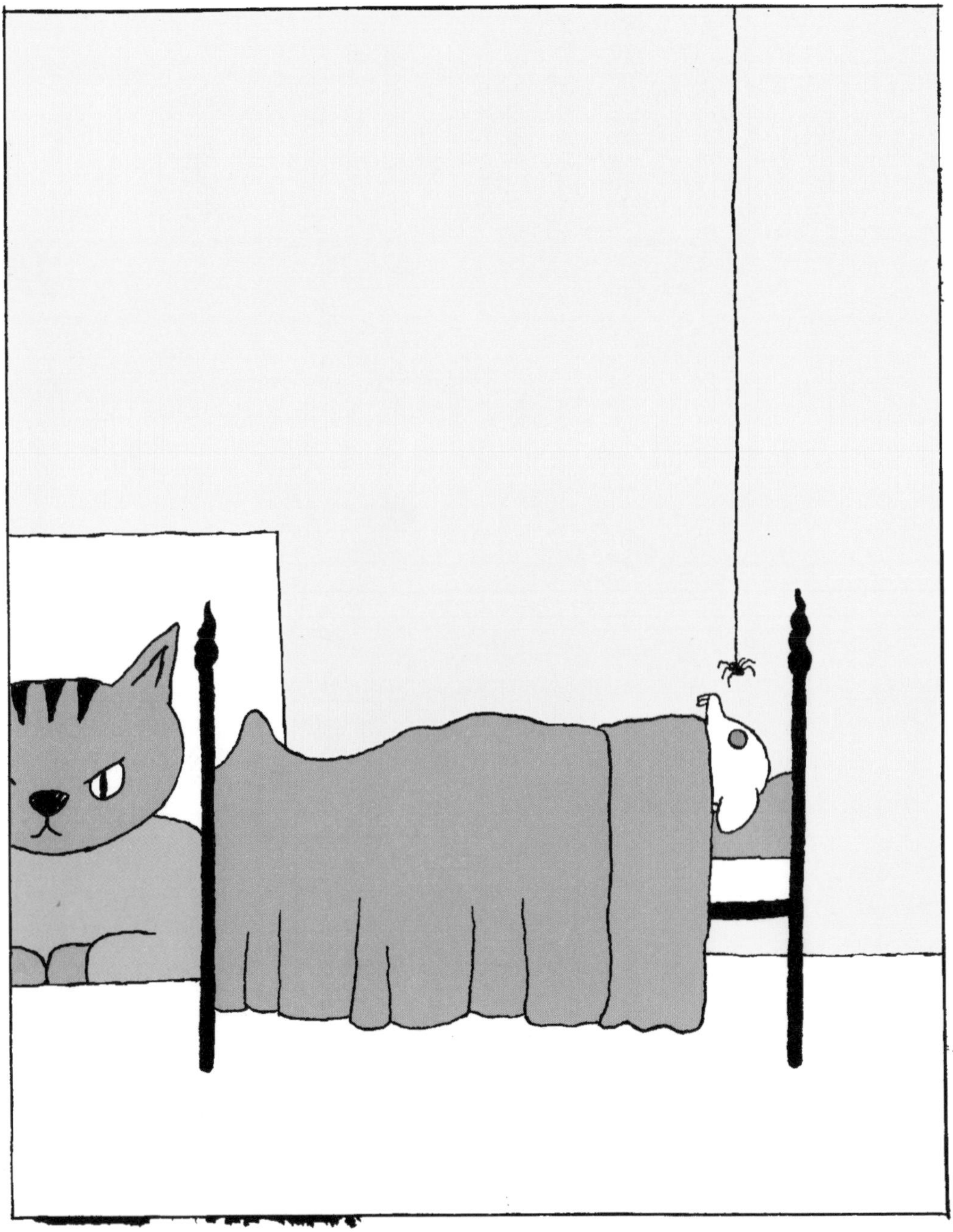

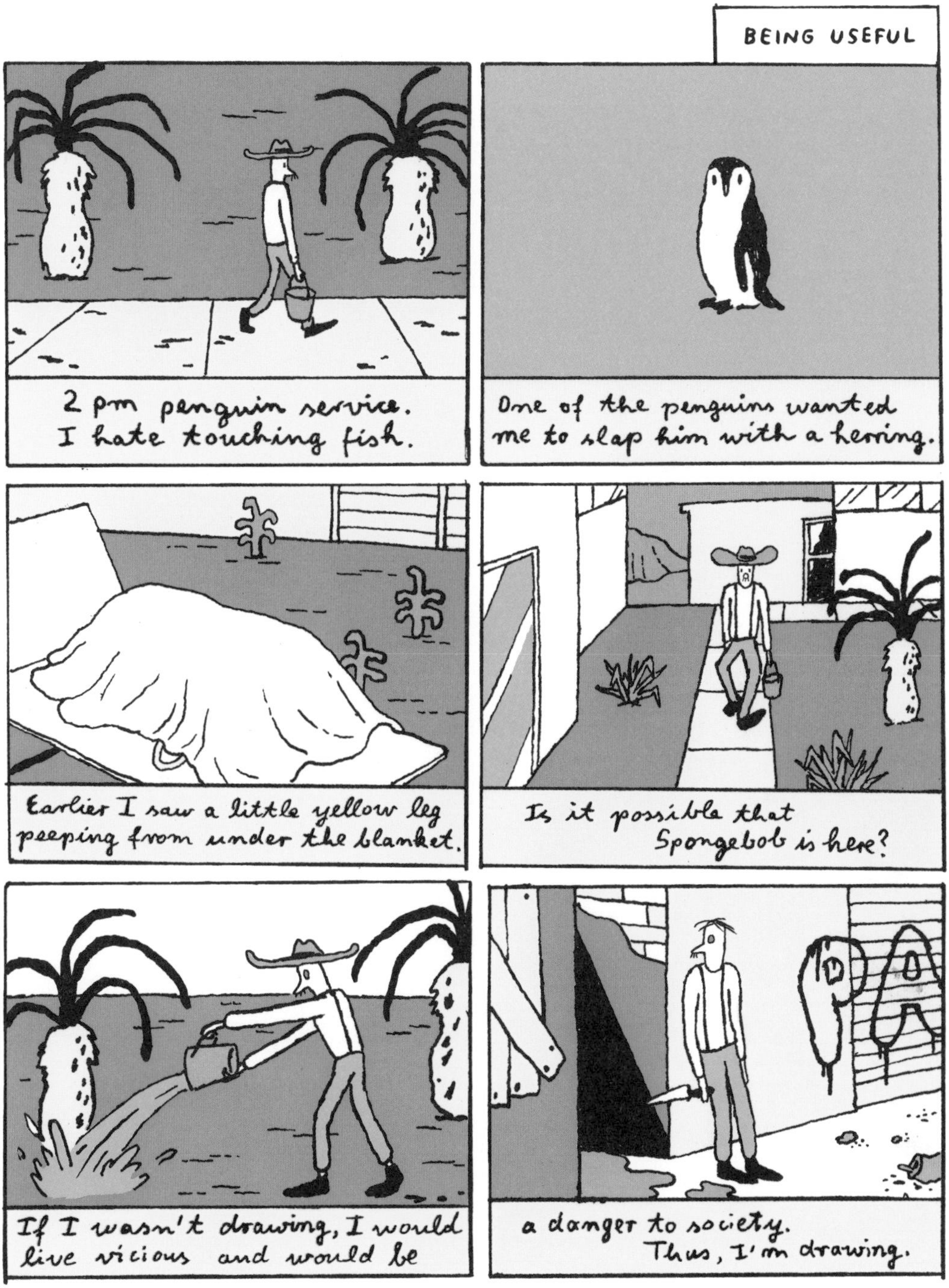
BEING USEFUL
2 pm penguin service. I hate touching fish.
One of the penguins wanted me to slap him with a herring.
Earlier I saw a little yellow leg peeping from under the blanket.
Is it possible that Spongebob is here?
If I wasn't drawing, I would live vicious and would be
a danger to society. Thus, I'm drawing.

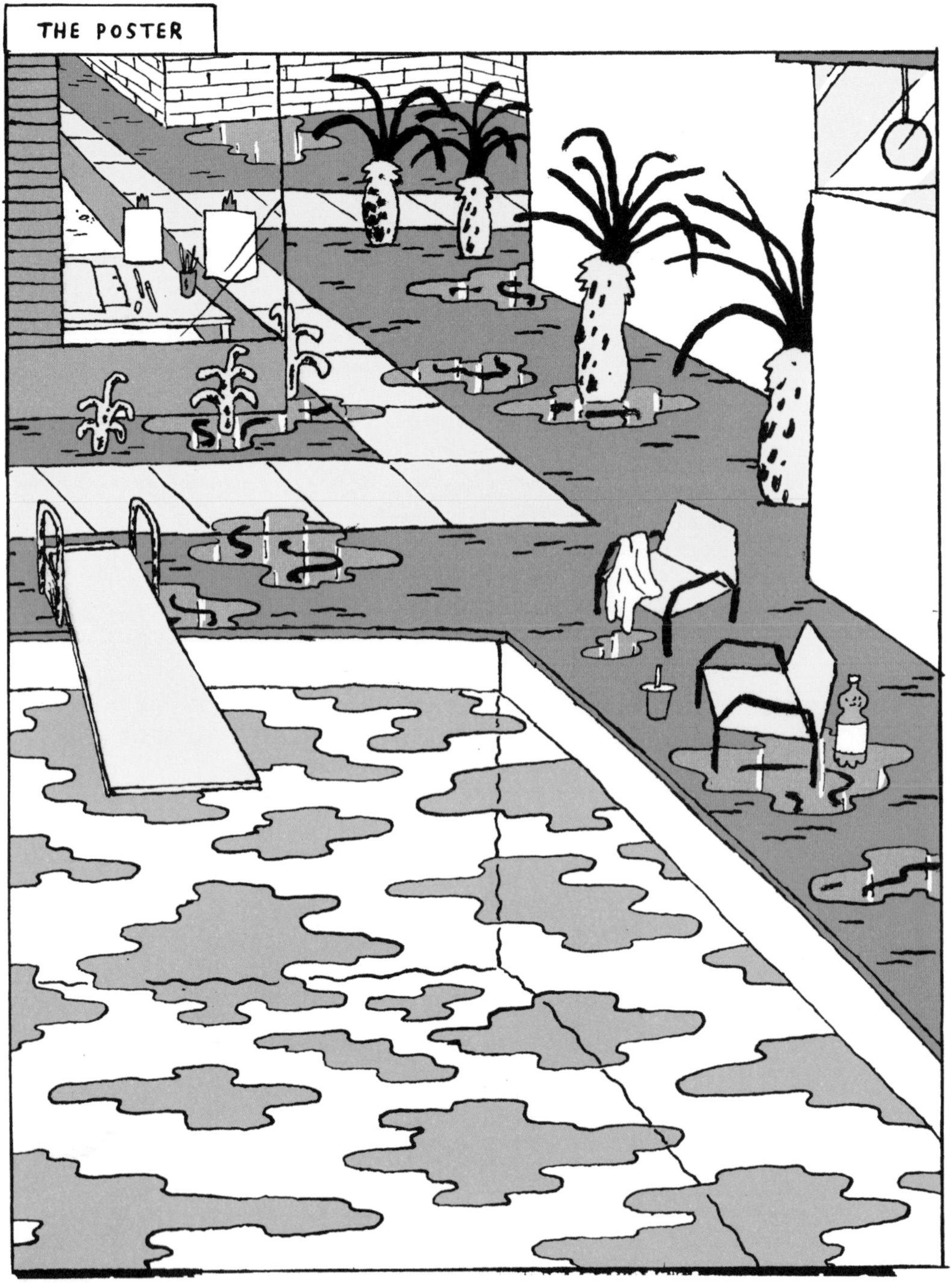
THE POSTER

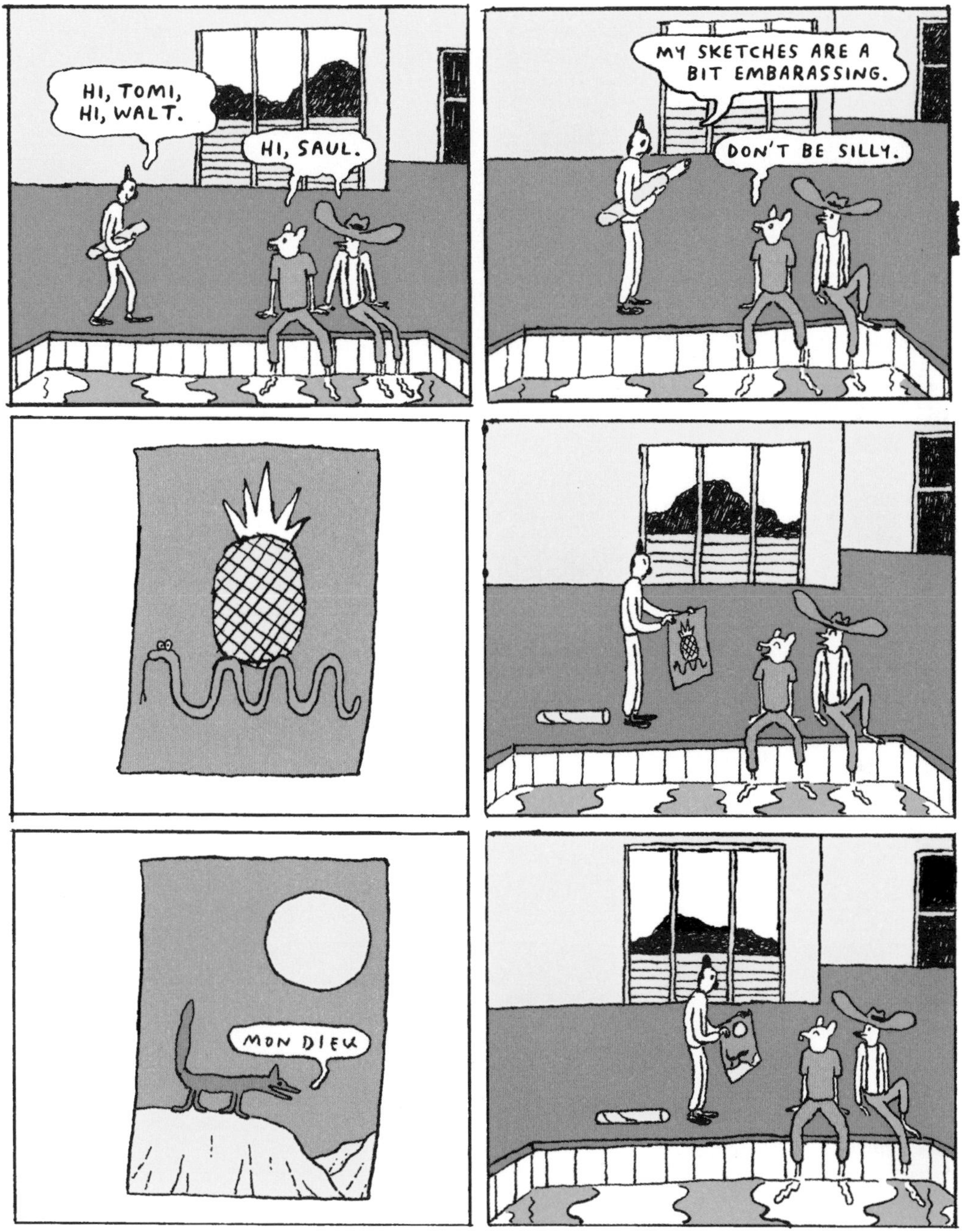
HI, TOMI,
HI, WALT.
HI, SAUL.
MY SKETCHES ARE A BIT EMBARASSING.
DON'T BE SILLY.
MON DIEU

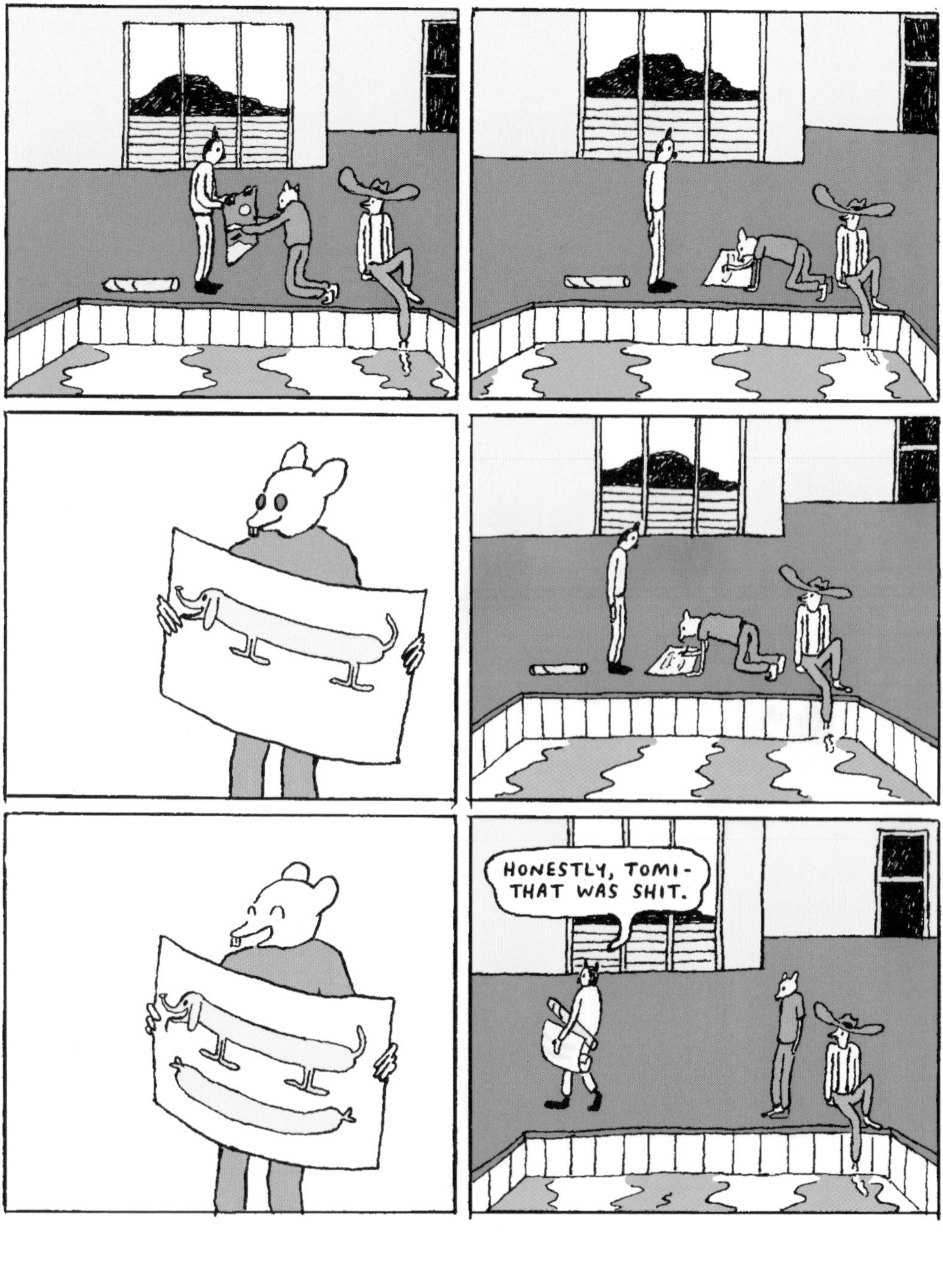
HONESTLY, TOMI-
THAT WAS SHIT.

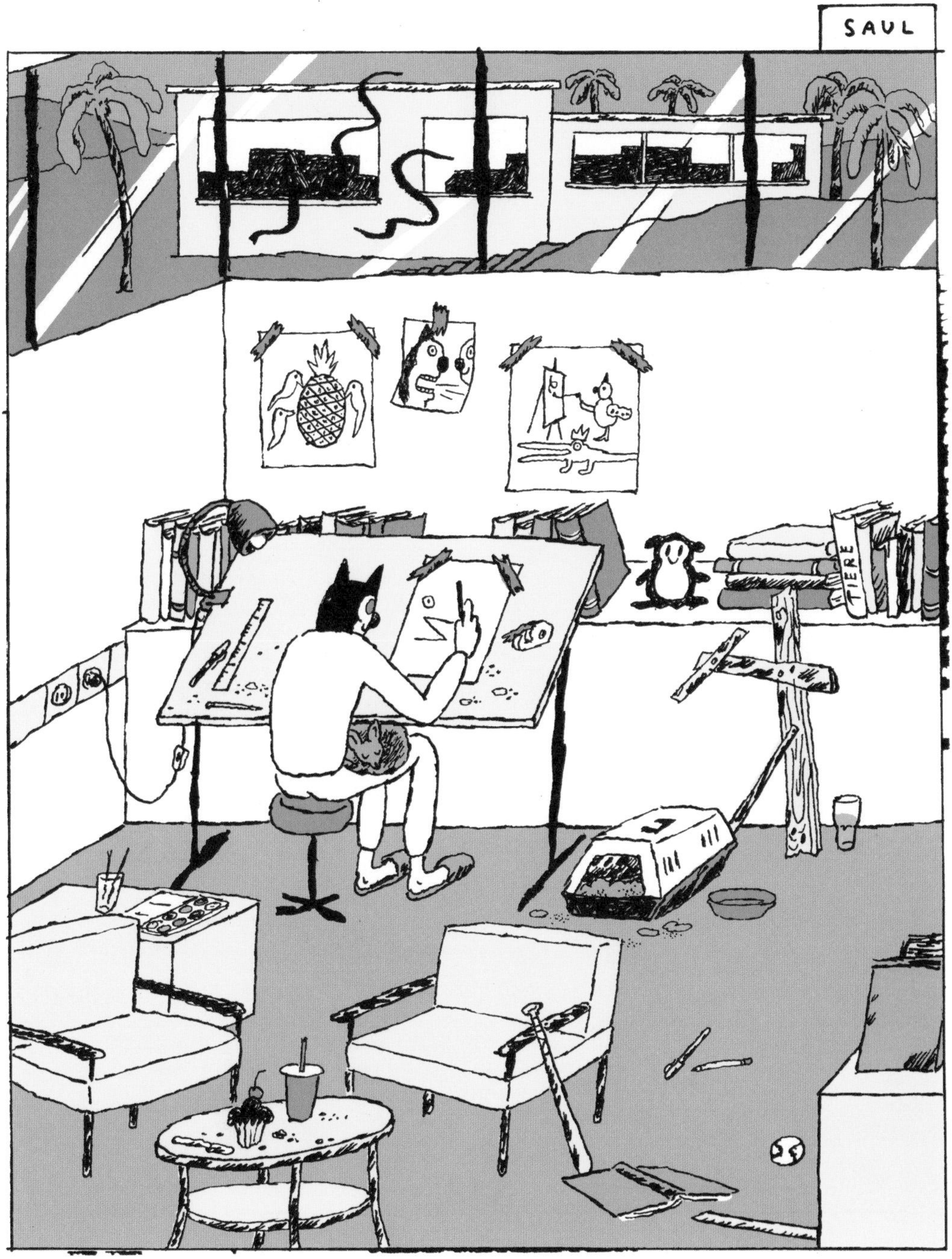
SAUL
TIERE

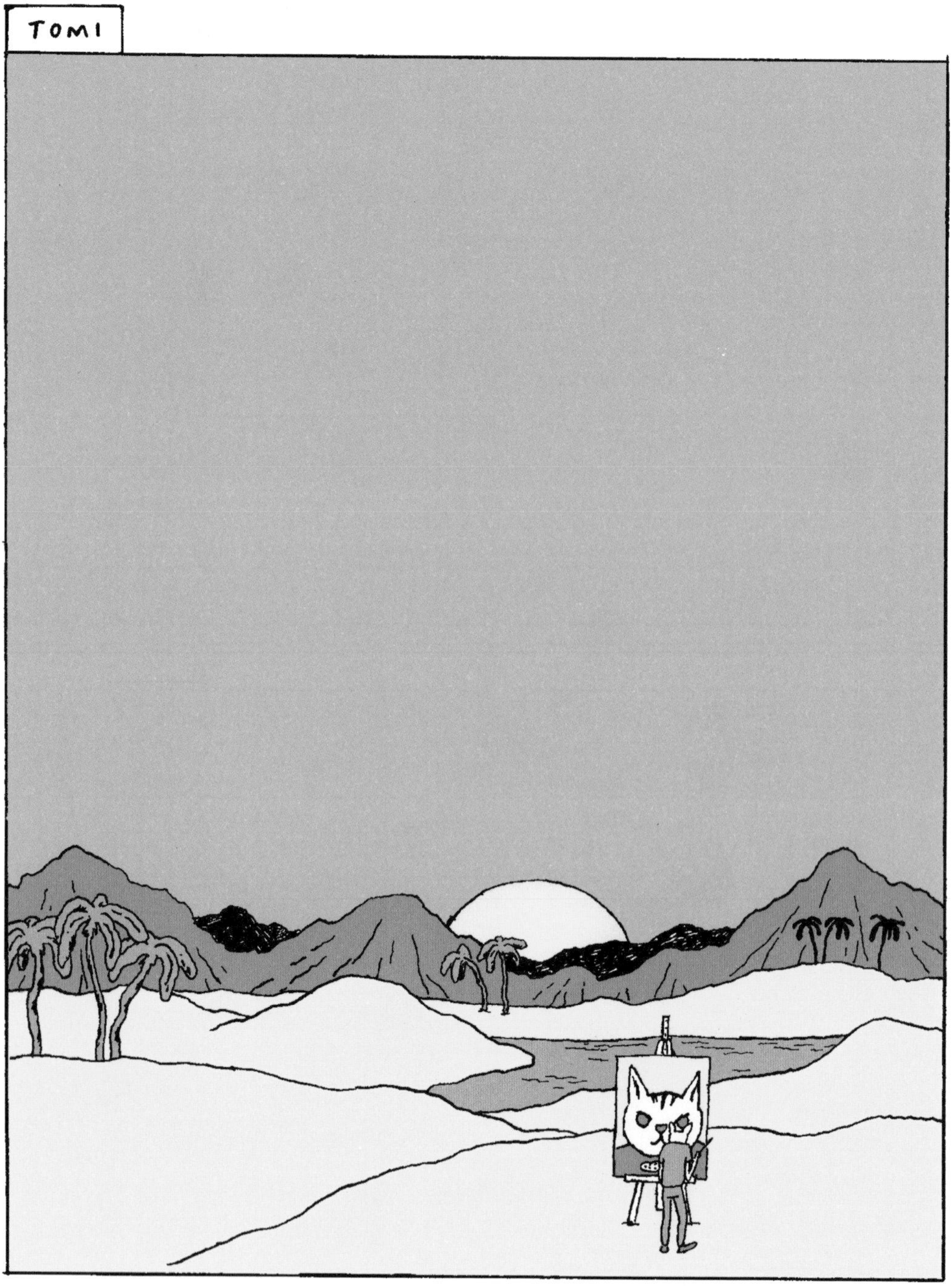
TOMI

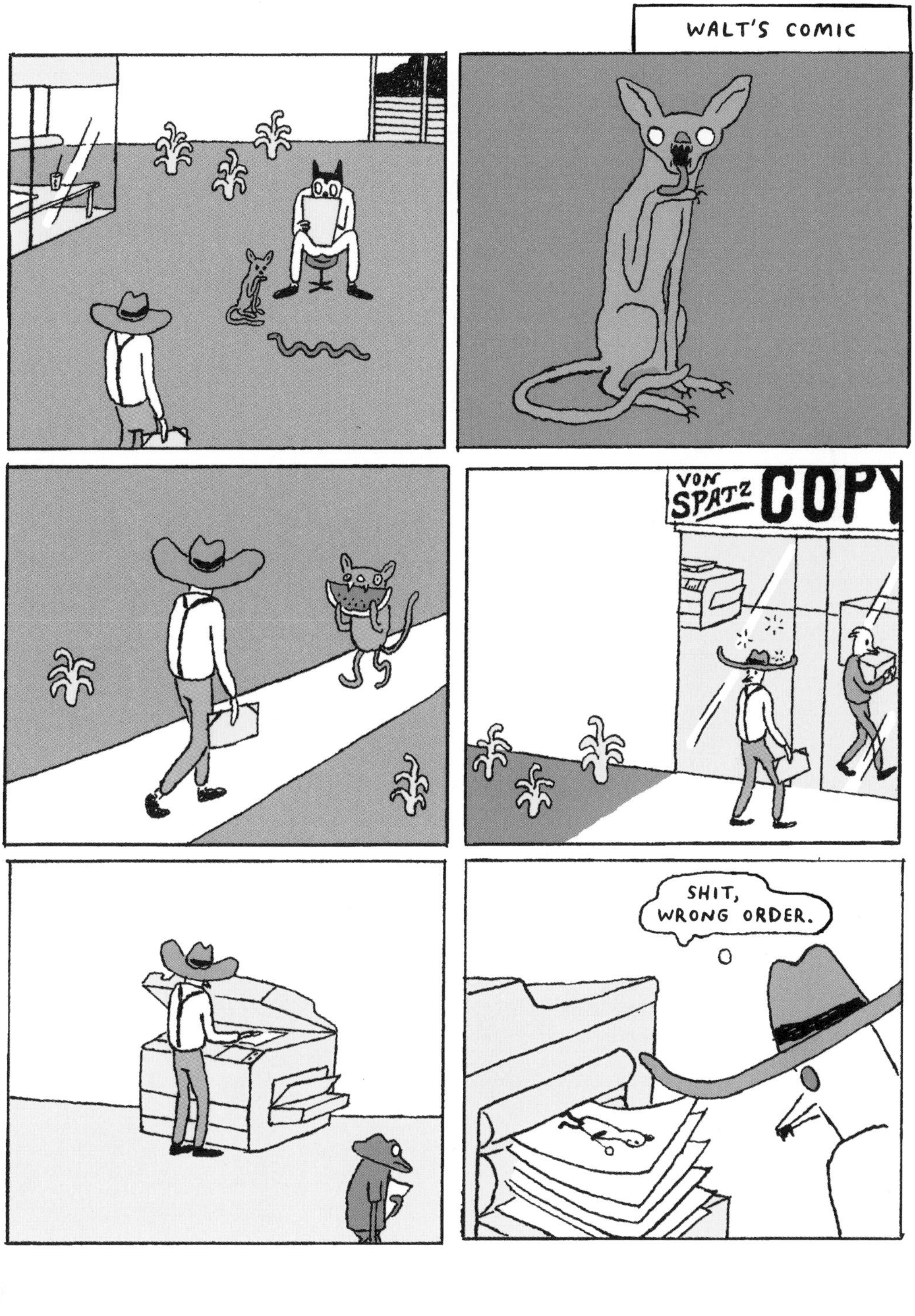
WALT'S COMIC
VON SPATZ COPY
SHIT, WRONG ORDER.

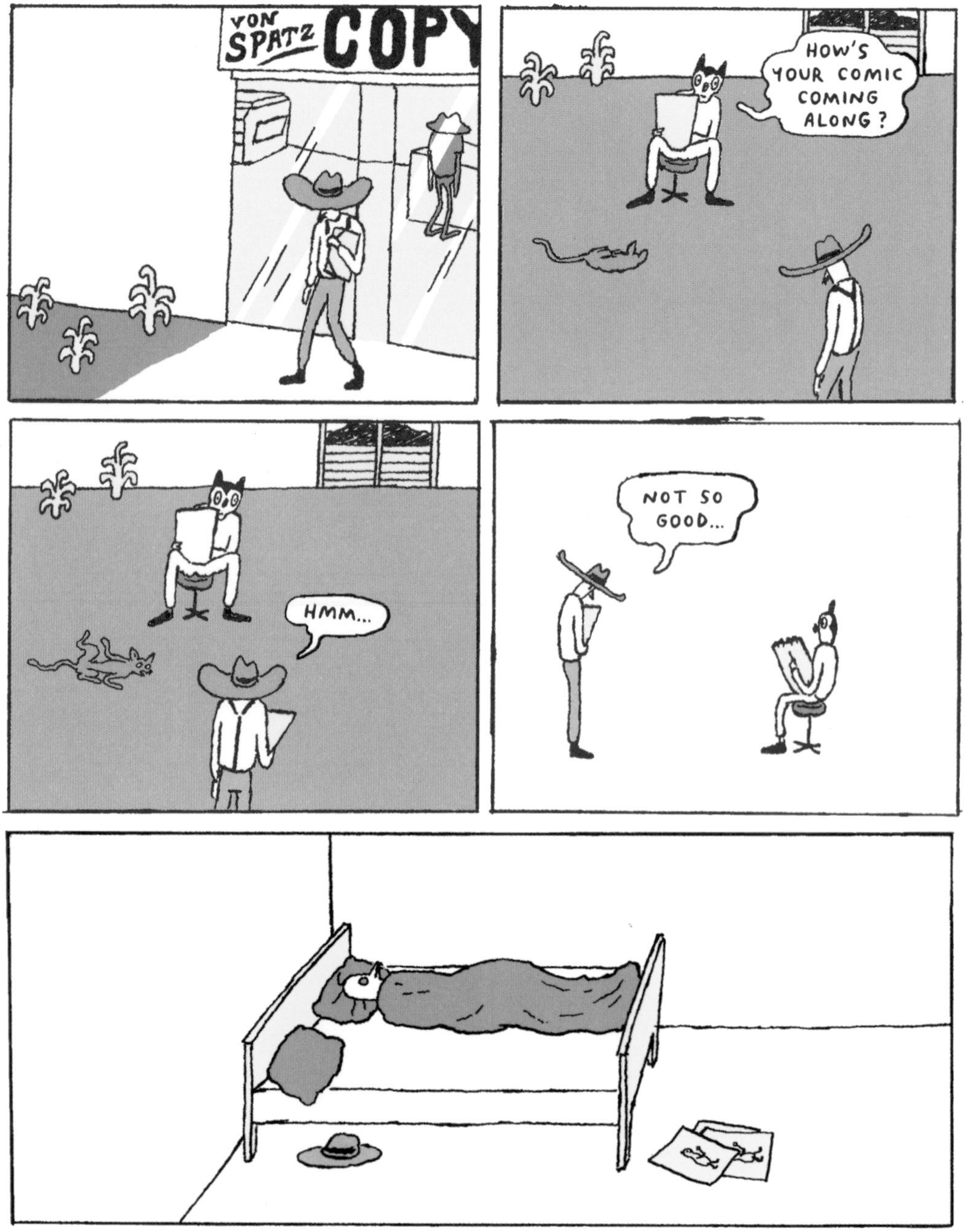
VON SPATZ COPY
HOW'S YOUR COMIC COMING ALONG?
HMM...
NOT SO GOOD...

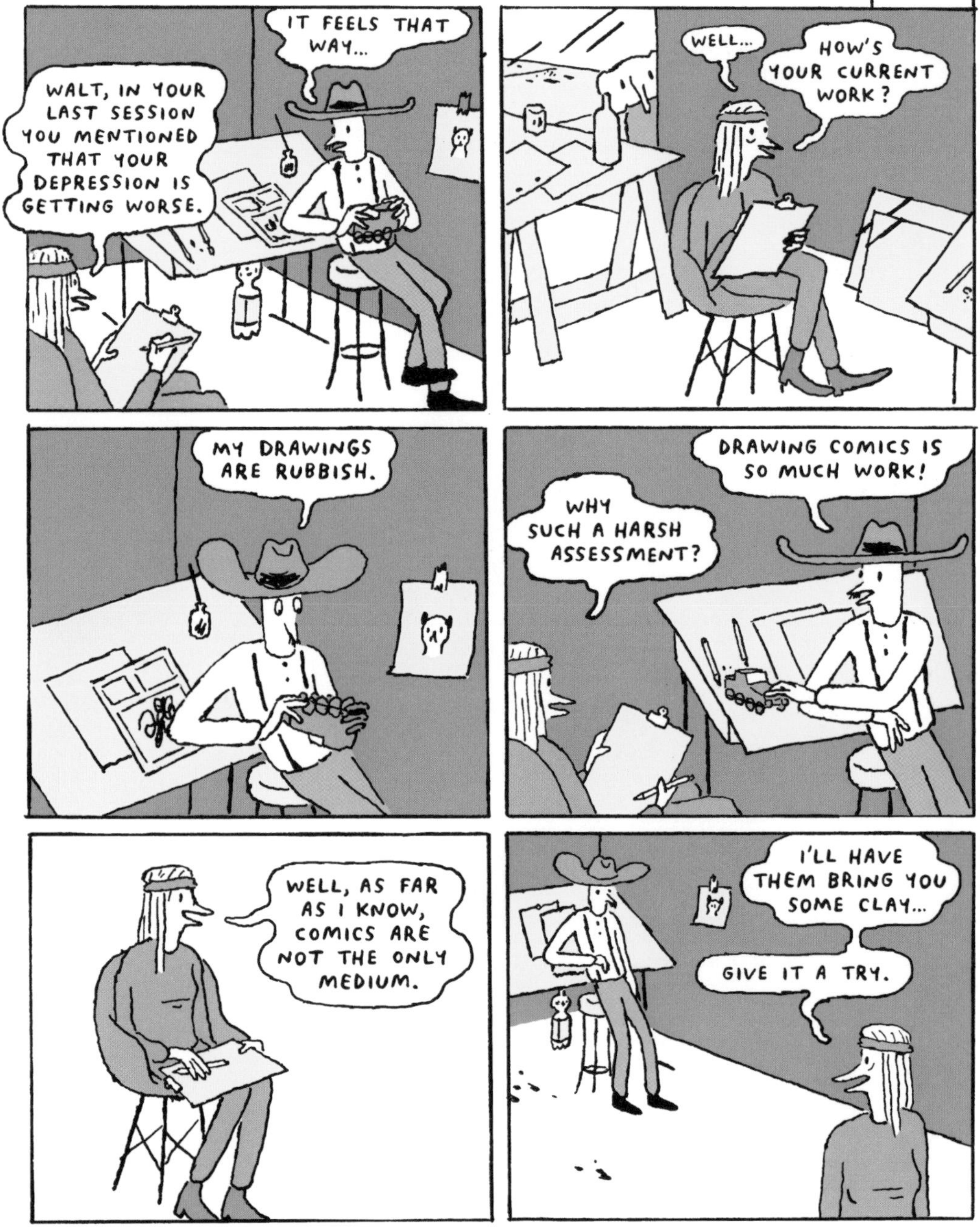
WALT, IN YOUR LAST SESSION YOU MENTIONED THAT YOUR DEPRESSION IS GETTING WORSE.
IT FEELS THAT WAY...
WELL...
HOW'S YOUR CURRENT WORK?
MY DRAWINGS ARE RUBBISH.
WHY SUCH A HARSH ASSESSMENT?
DRAWING COMICS IS SO MUCH WORK!
WELL, AS FAR AS I KNOW, COMICS ARE NOT THE ONLY MEDIUM.
I'LL HAVE THEM BRING YOU SOME CLAY...
GIVE IT A TRY.

PROZAC©

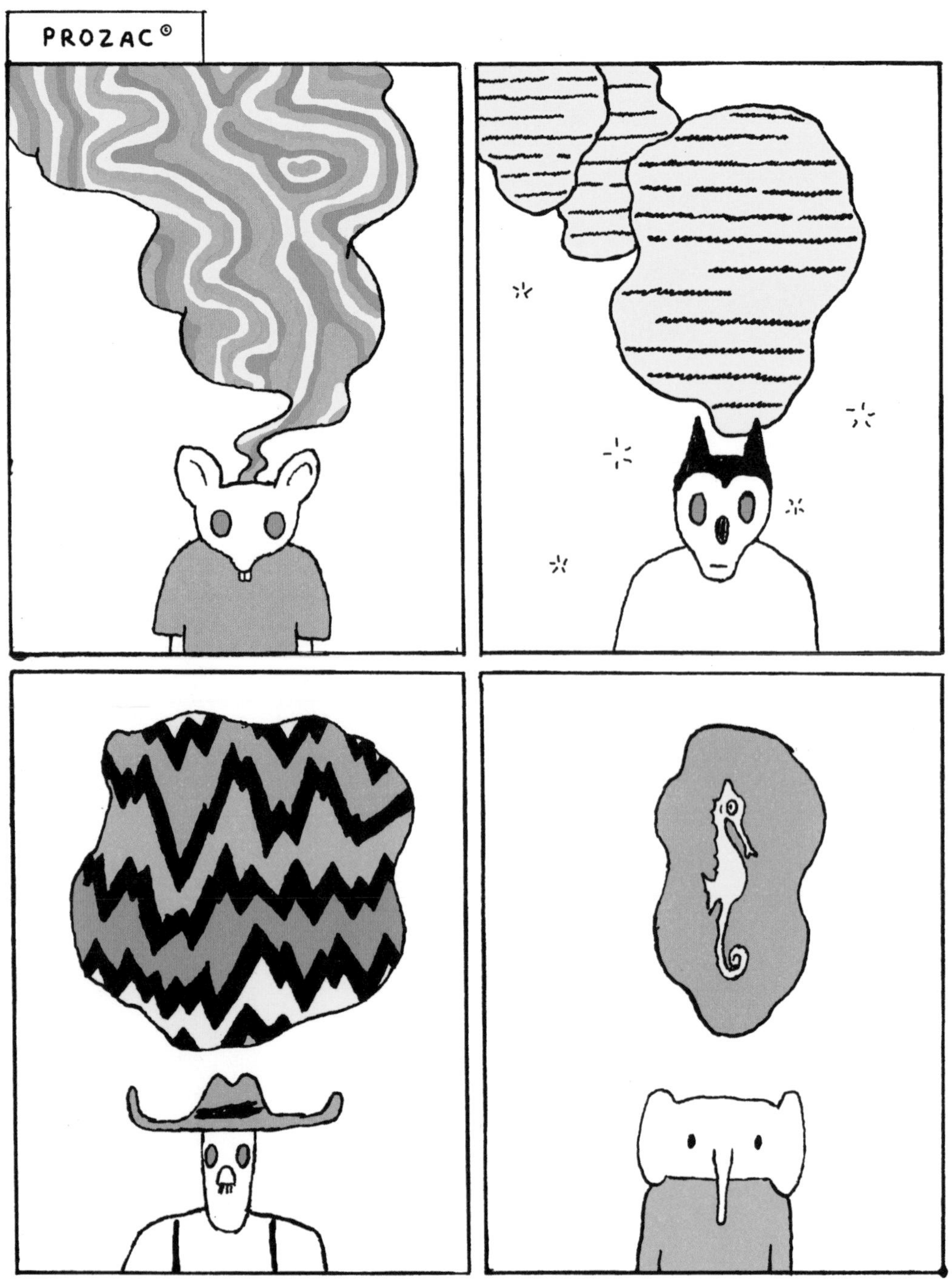

FALCONRY

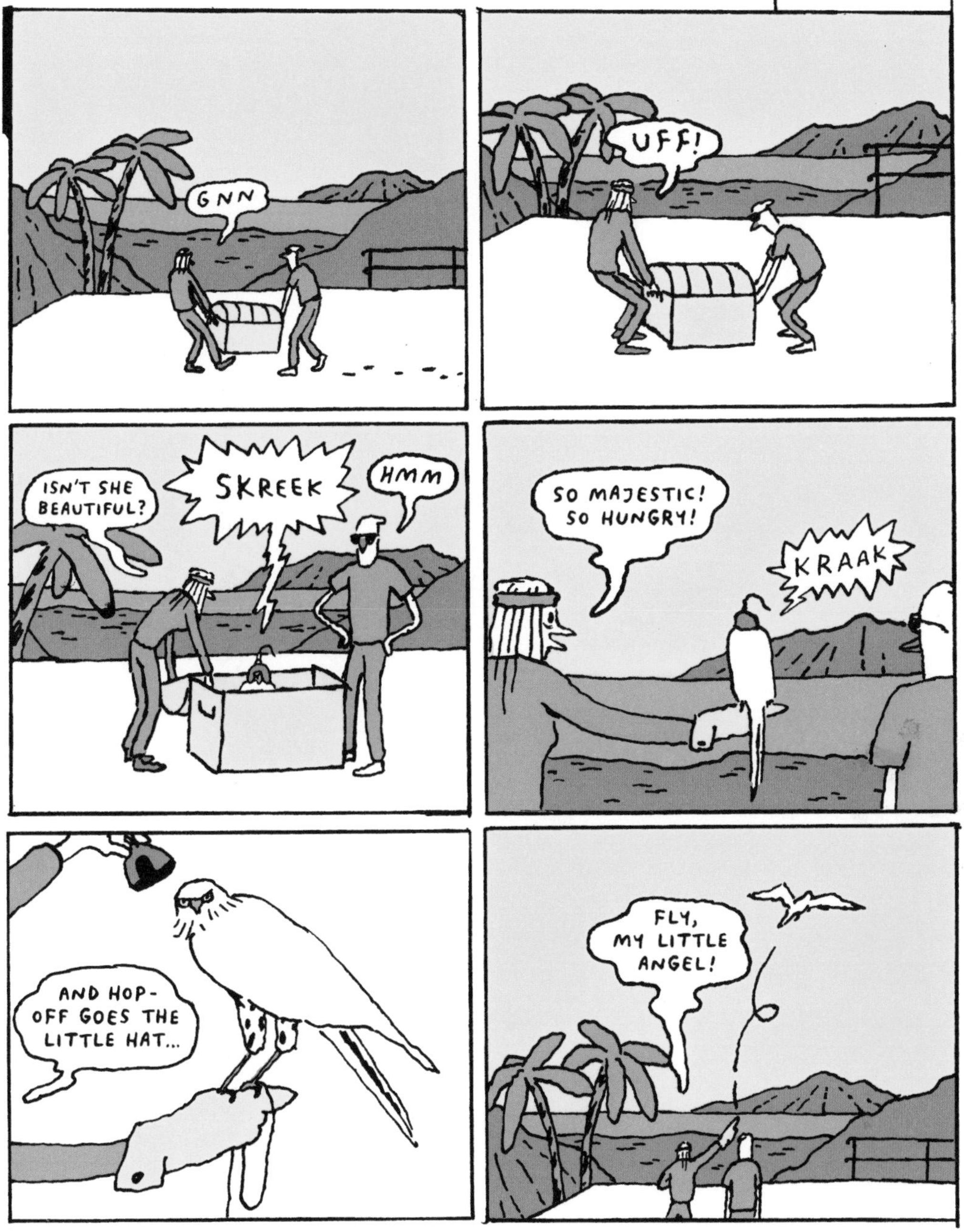
GNN
UFF!
ISN'T SHE BEAUTIFUL?
SKREEK
HMM
SO MAJESTIC! SO HUNGRY!
KRAAK
AND HOP-OFF GOES THE LITTLE HAT...
FLY, MY LITTLE ANGEL!

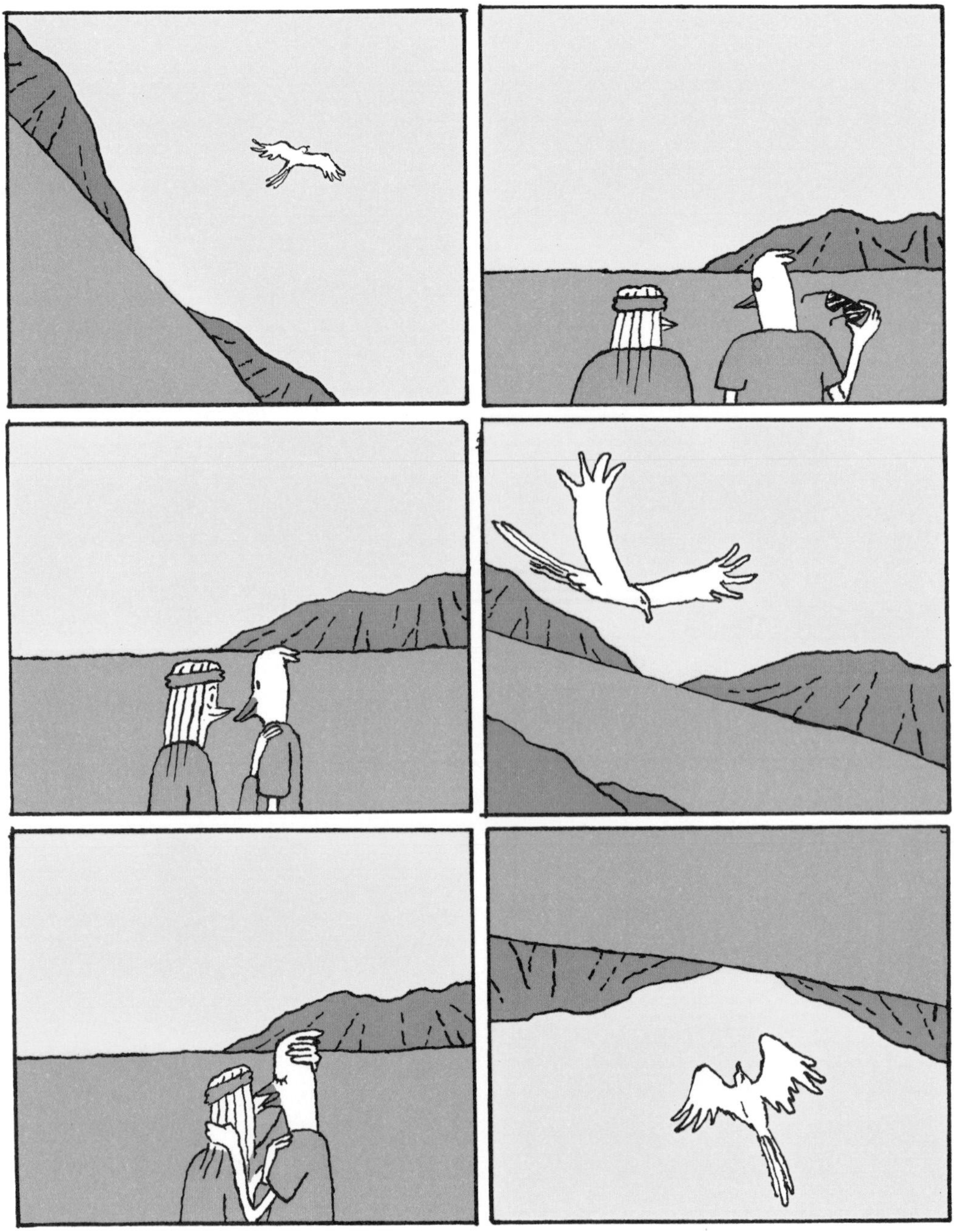

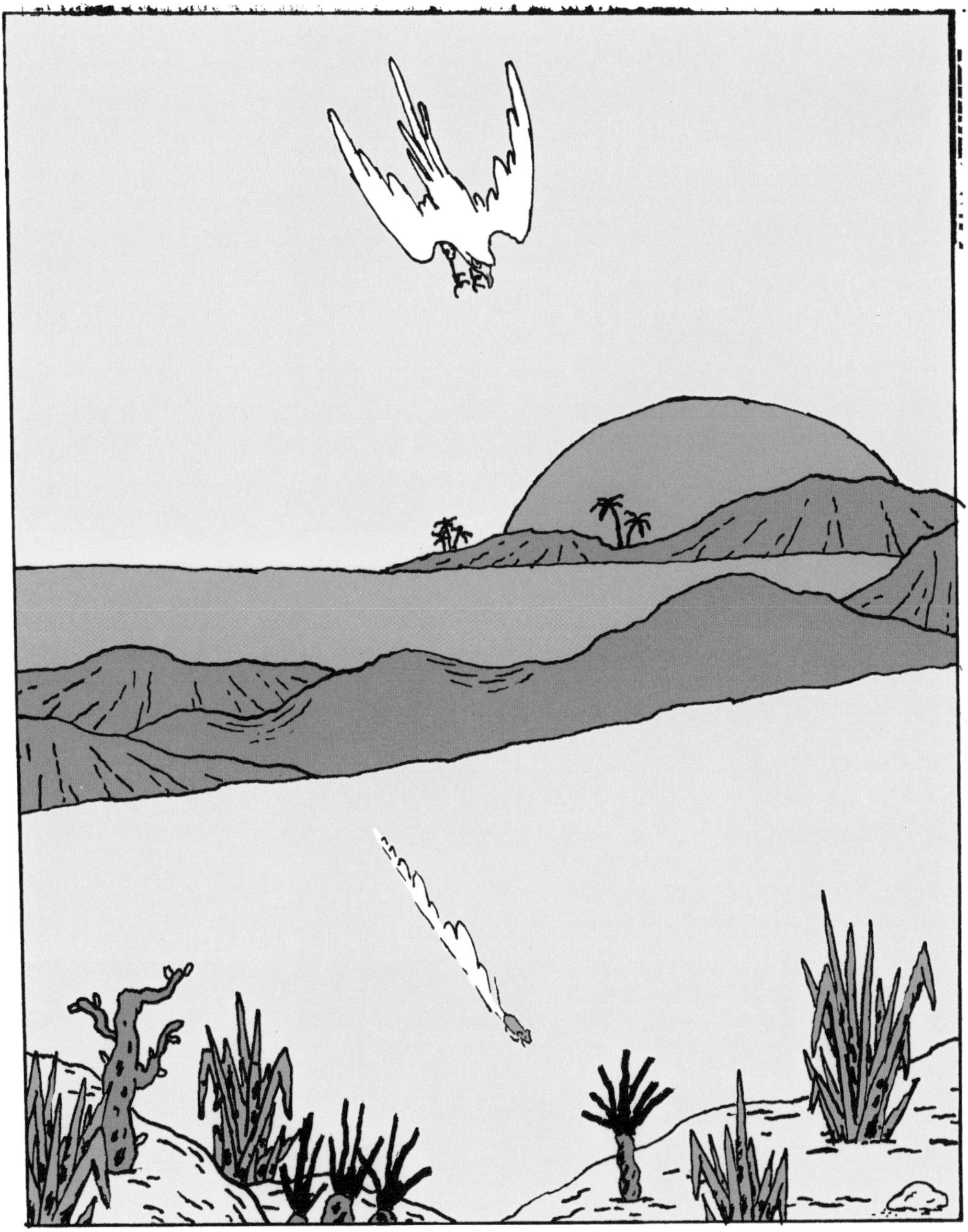

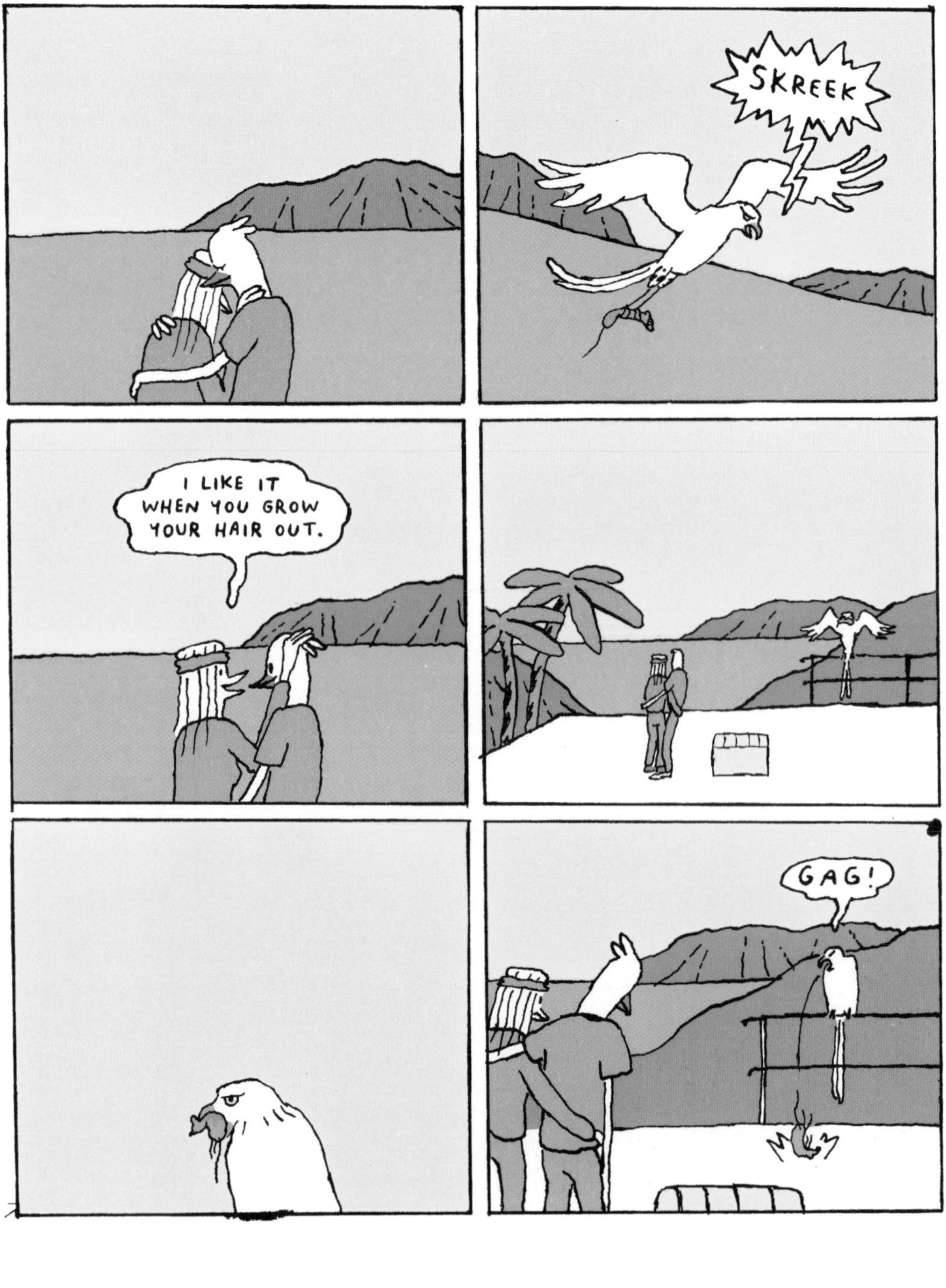
SKREEK
I LIKE IT WHEN YOU GROW YOUR HAIR OUT.
GAG!

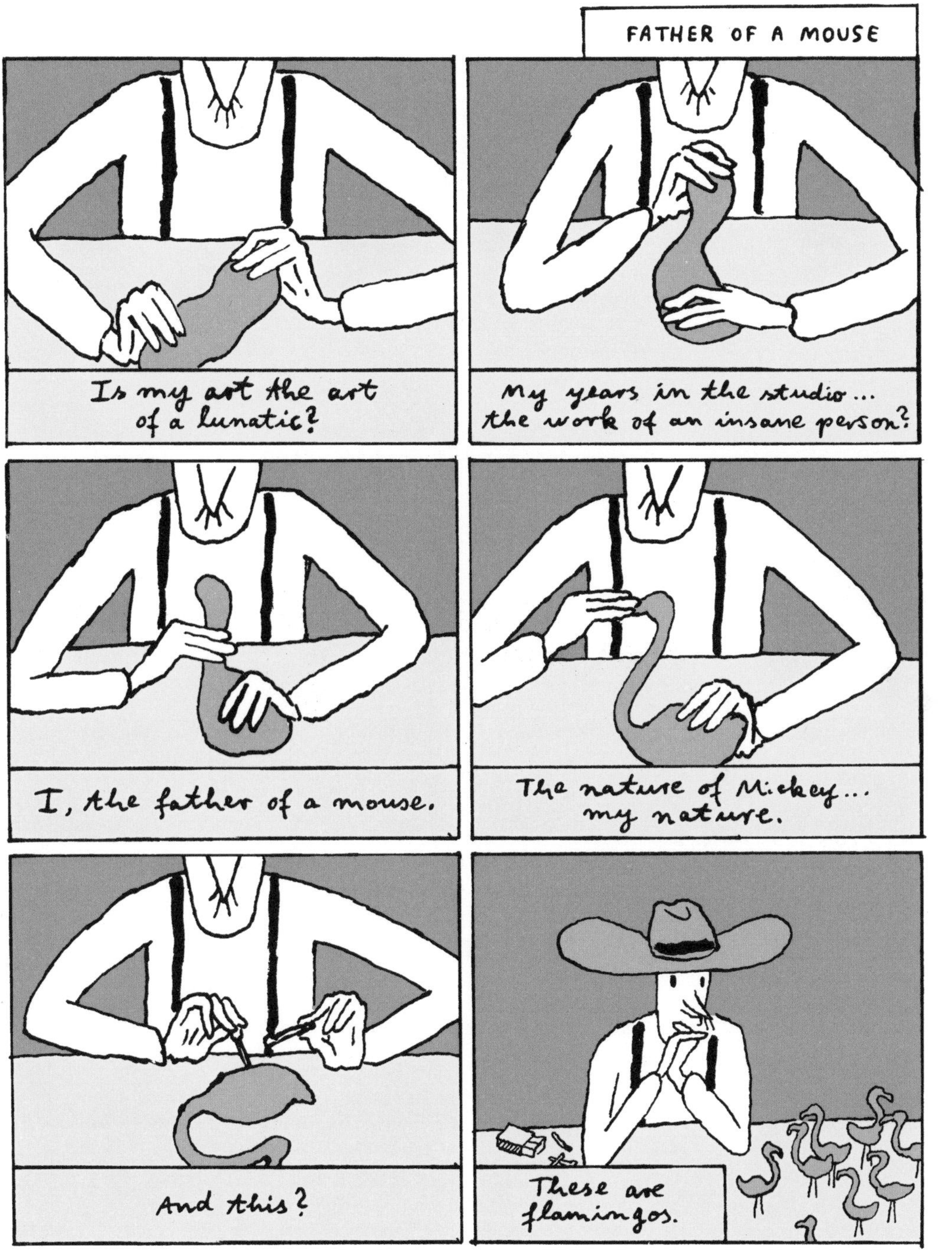
FATHER OF A MOUSE
Is my art the art of a lunatic?
My years in the studio... the work of an insane person?
I, the father of a mouse.
The nature of Mickey... my nature.
And this?
These are flamingos.

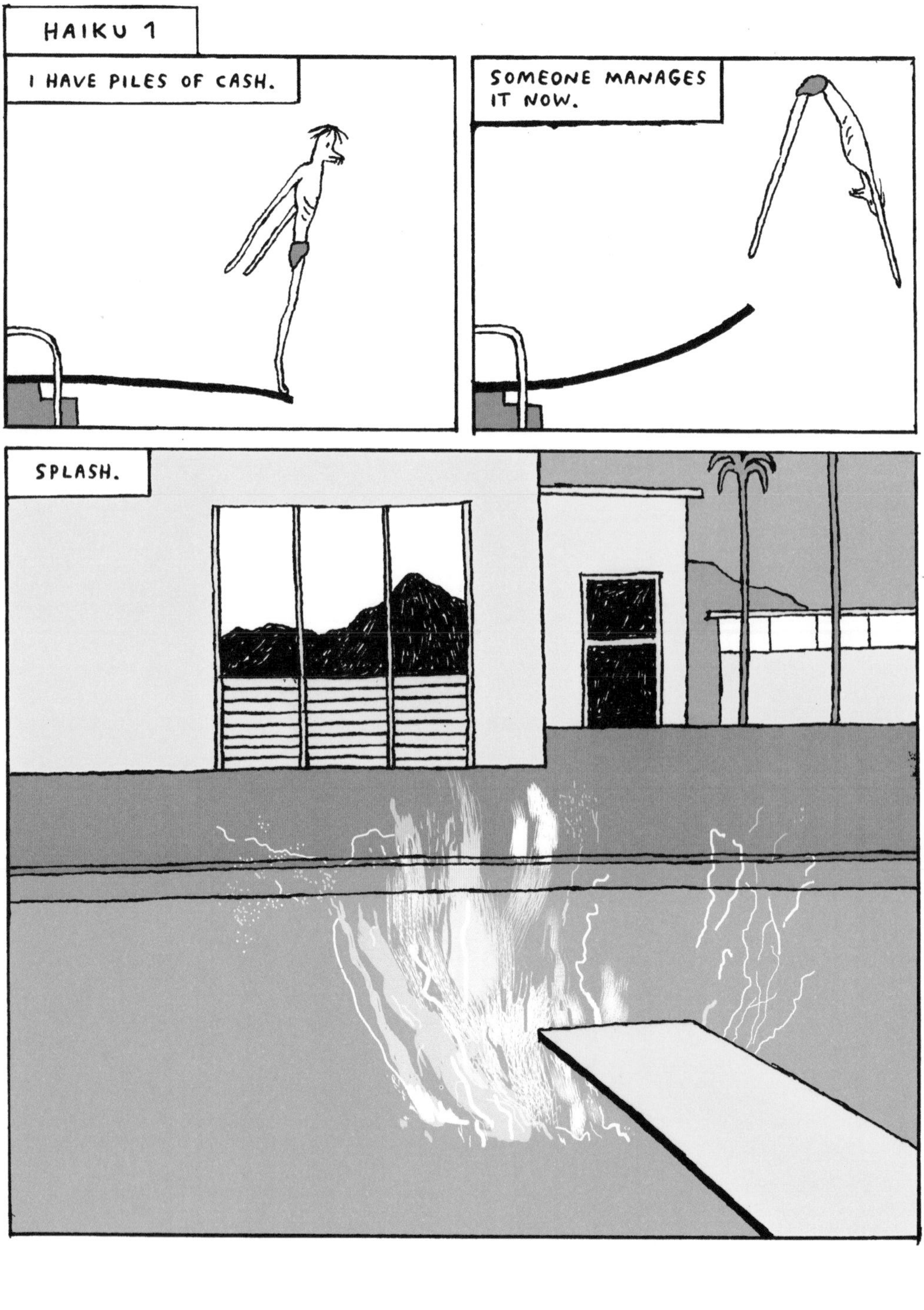
HAIKU 1
I HAVE PILES OF CASH.
SOMEONE MANAGES IT NOW.
SPLASH.

LEISURE

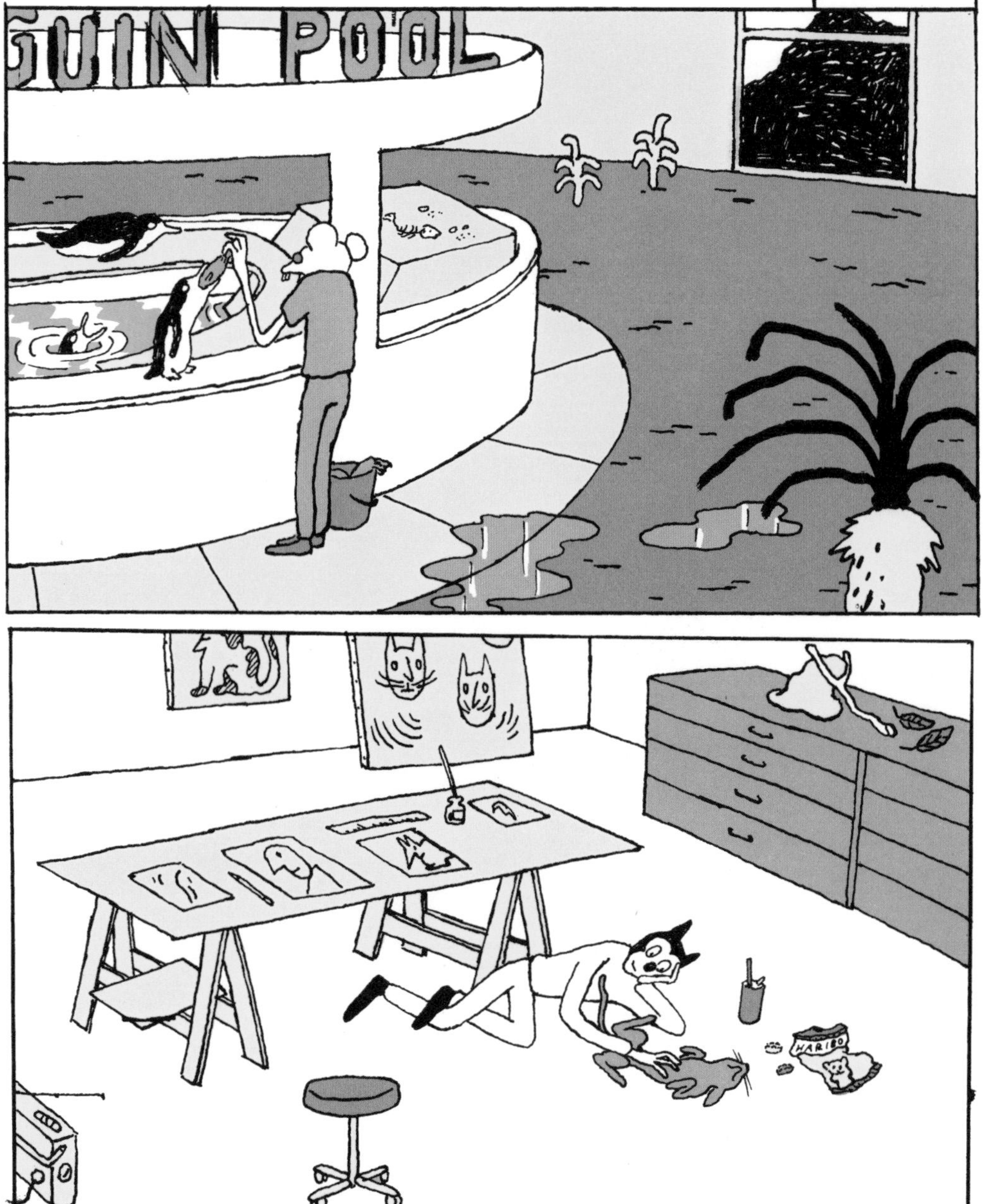
GUIN POOL
HARIBO

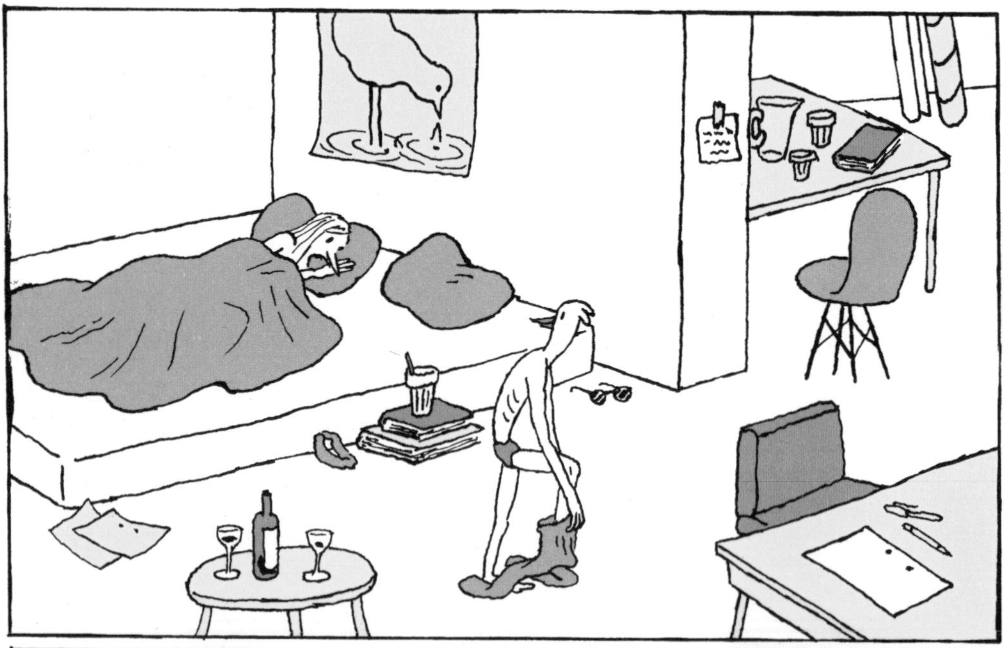

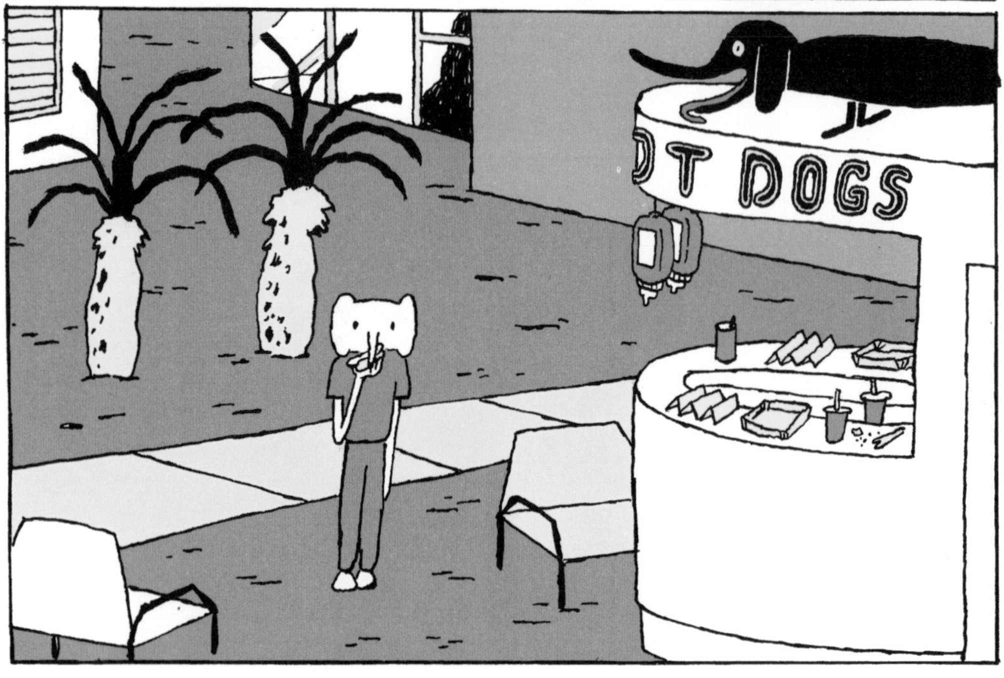

DOGS

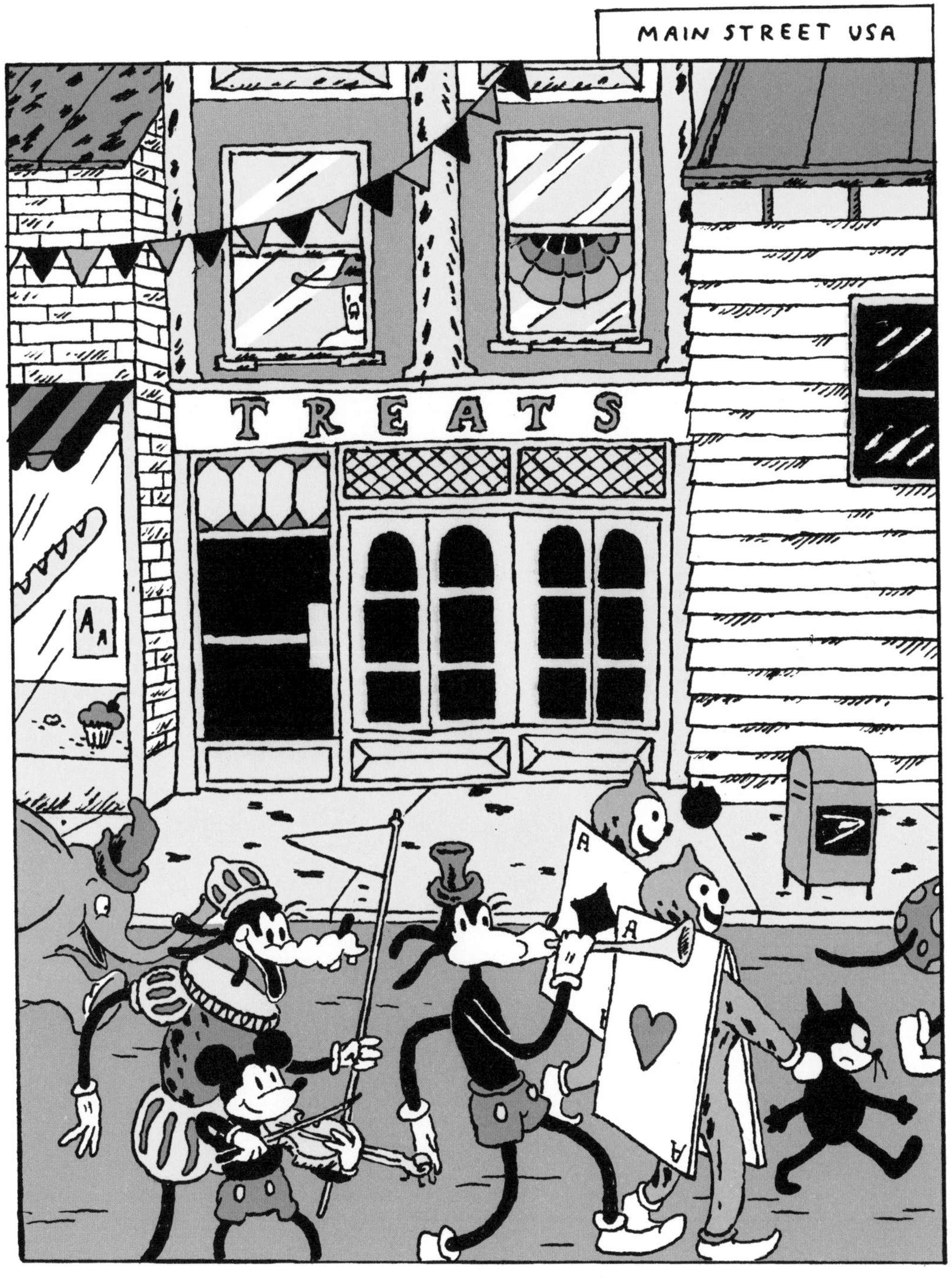
MAIN STREET USA
TREATS

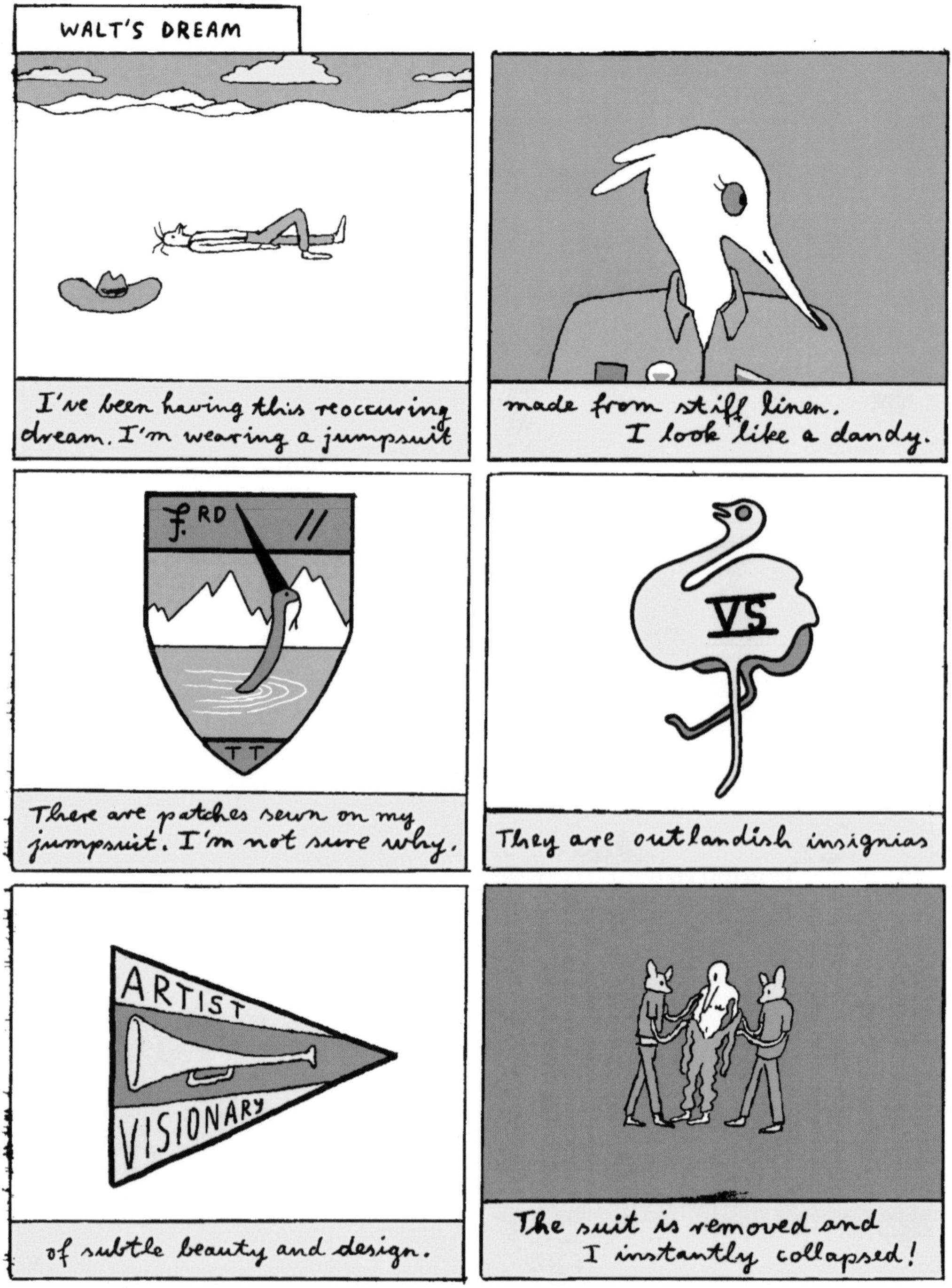
WALT'S DREAM
I've been having this reoccuring dream. I'm wearing a jumpsuit
made from stiff linen. I look like a dandy.
F. RD //
TT
There are patches sewn on my jumpsuit. I'm not sure why.
VS
They are outlandish insignias
ARTIST
VISIONARY
of subtle beauty and design.
The suit is removed and I instantly collapsed!

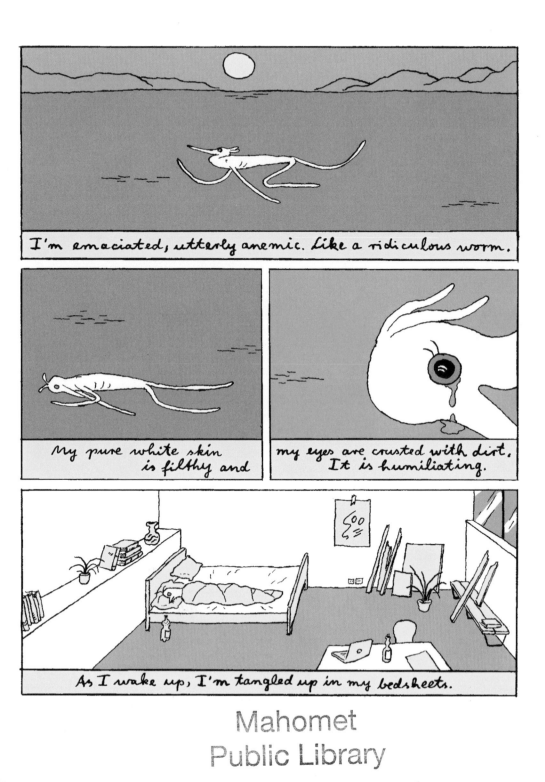

I'm emaciated, utterly anemic. Like a ridiculous worm.

My pure white skin is filthy and

my eyes are crusted with dirt. It is humiliating.

As I wake up, I'm tangled up in my bedsheets.

THE EXHIBITION

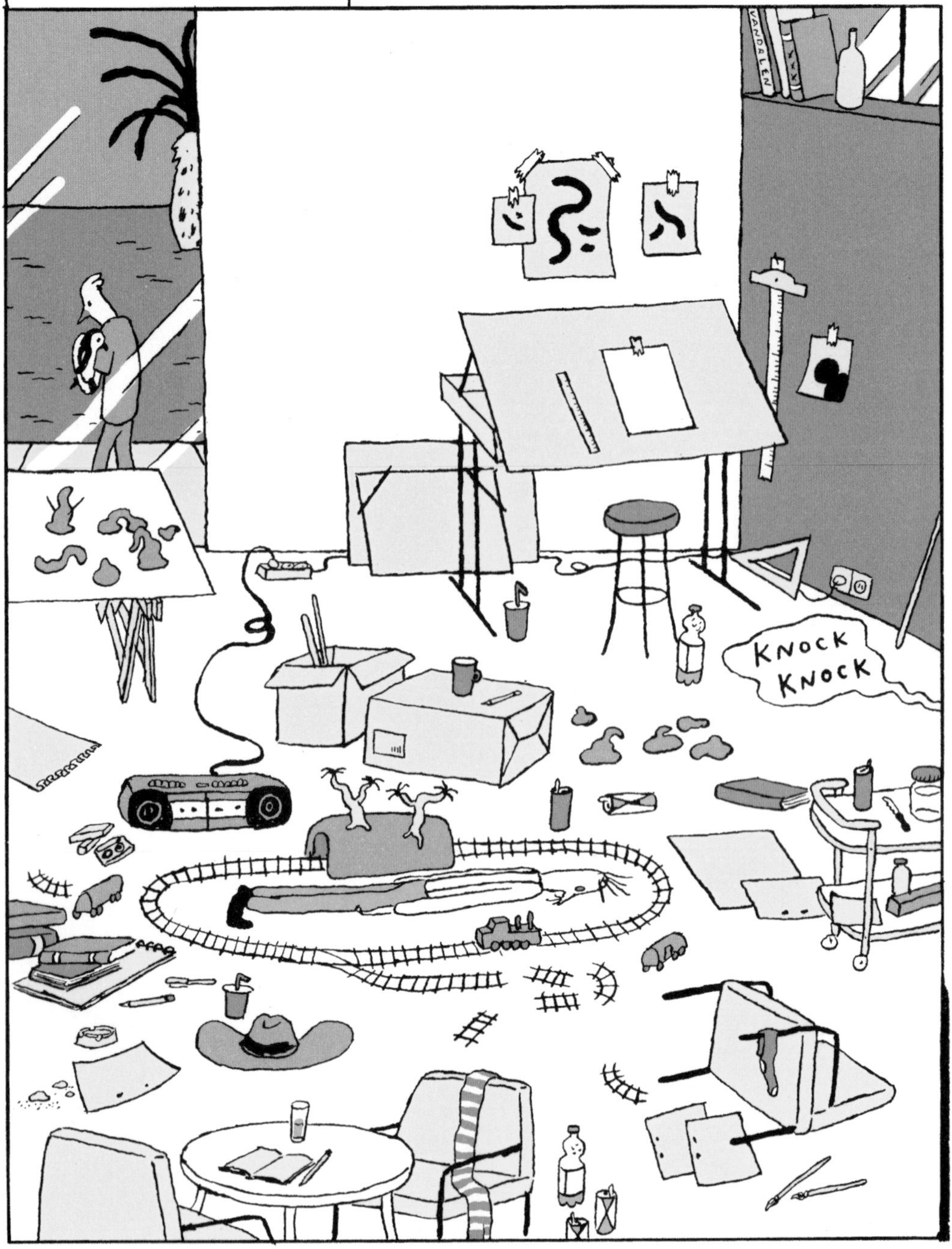
VANDALEN
KNOCK KNOCK

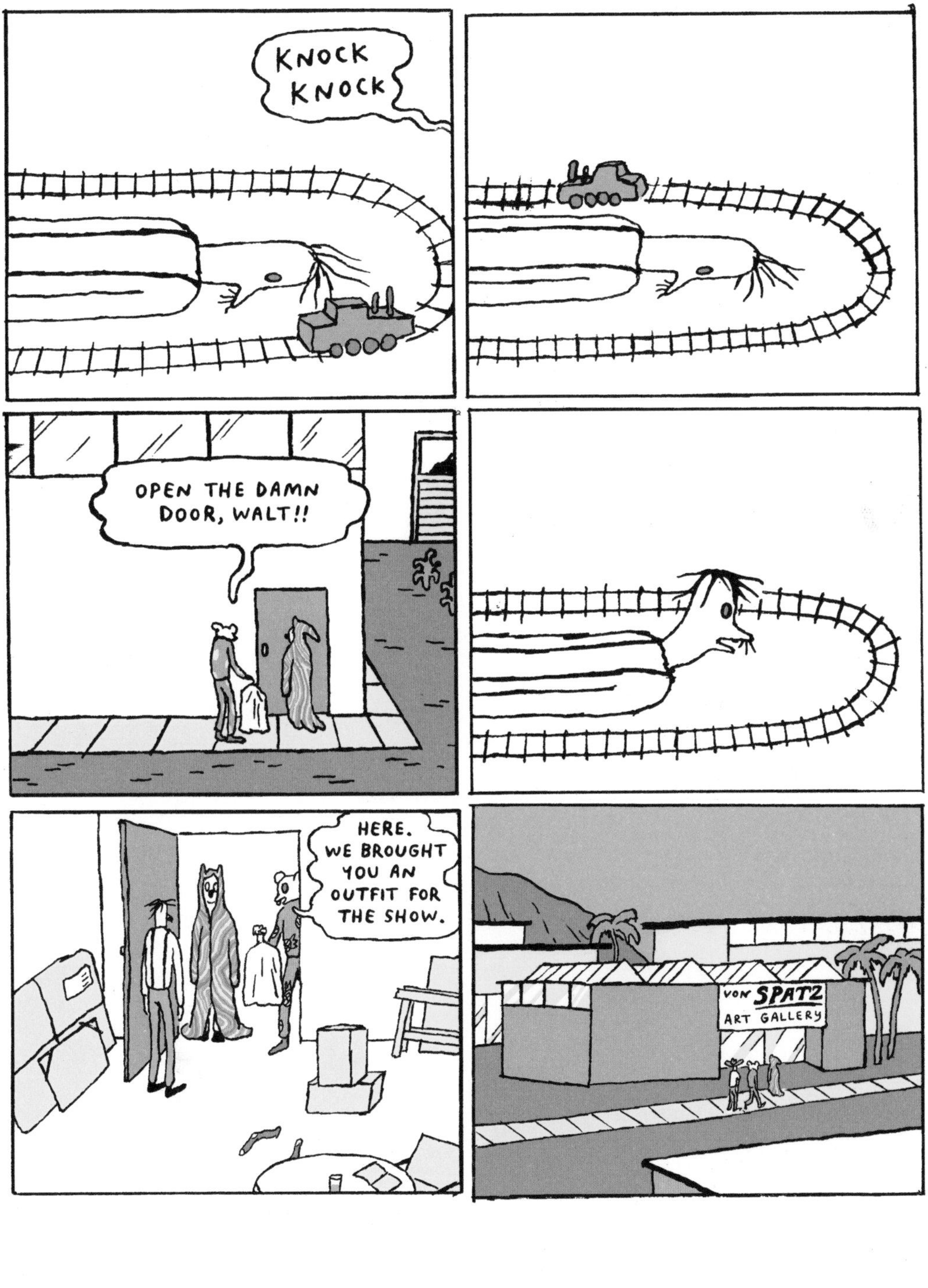
KNOCK KNOCK
OPEN THE DAMN DOOR, WALT!!
HERE. WE BROUGHT YOU AN OUTFIT FOR THE SHOW.
VON SPATZ ART GALLERY

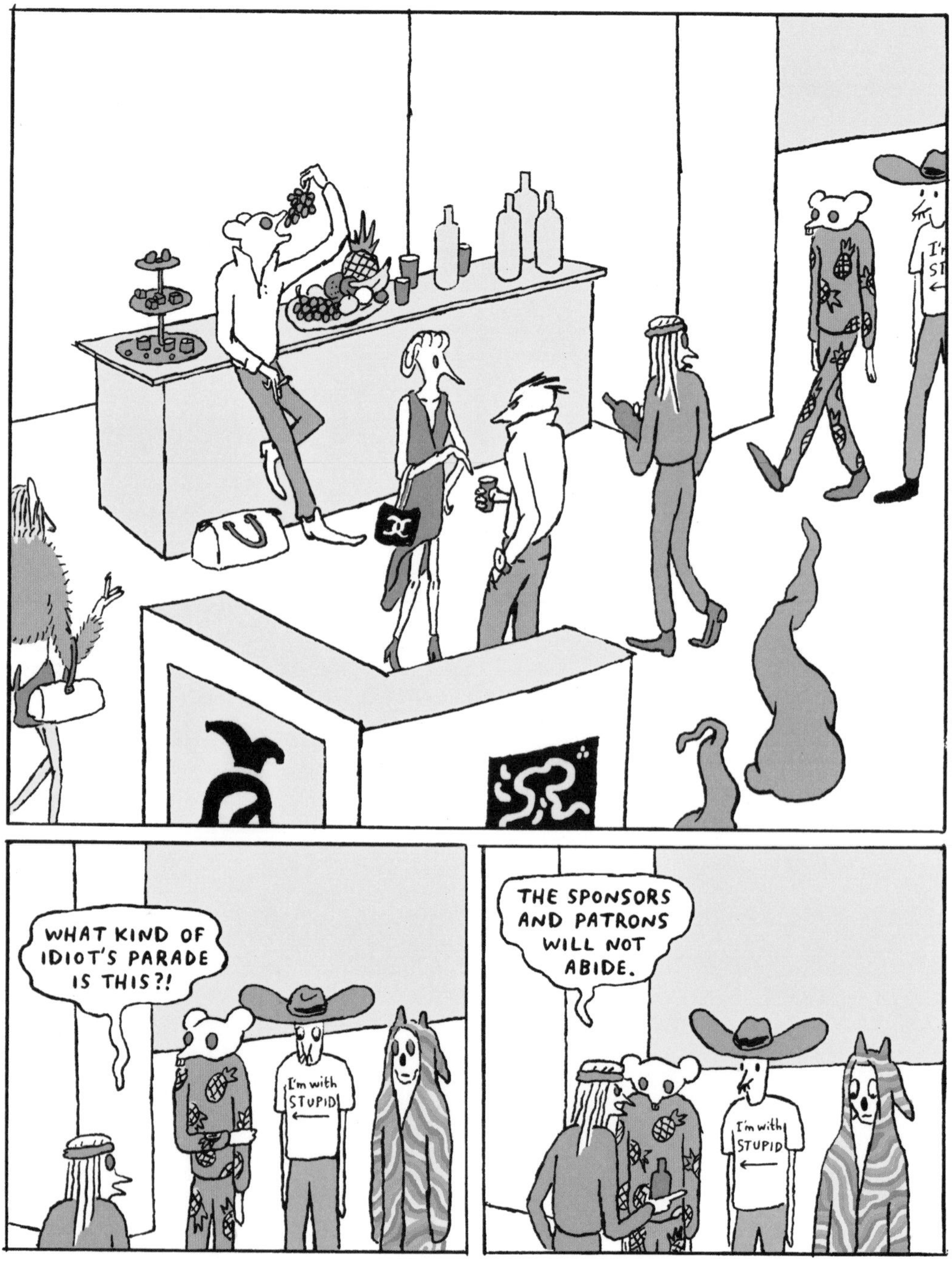
I'm with ST
WHAT KIND OF IDIOT'S PARADE IS THIS?!
I'm with STUPID
THE SPONSORS AND PATRONS WILL NOT ABIDE.
I'm with STUPID

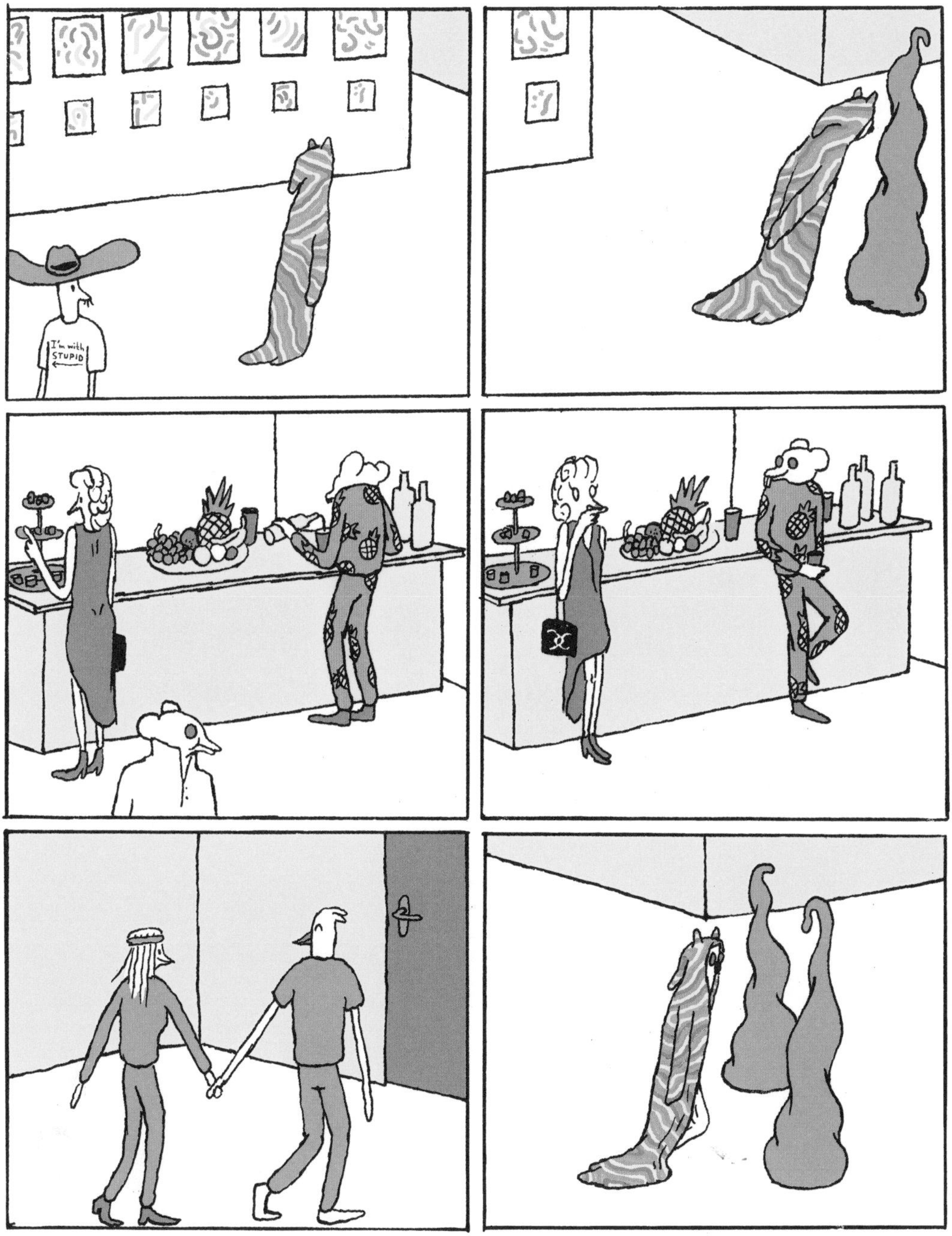
I'm with
STUPID

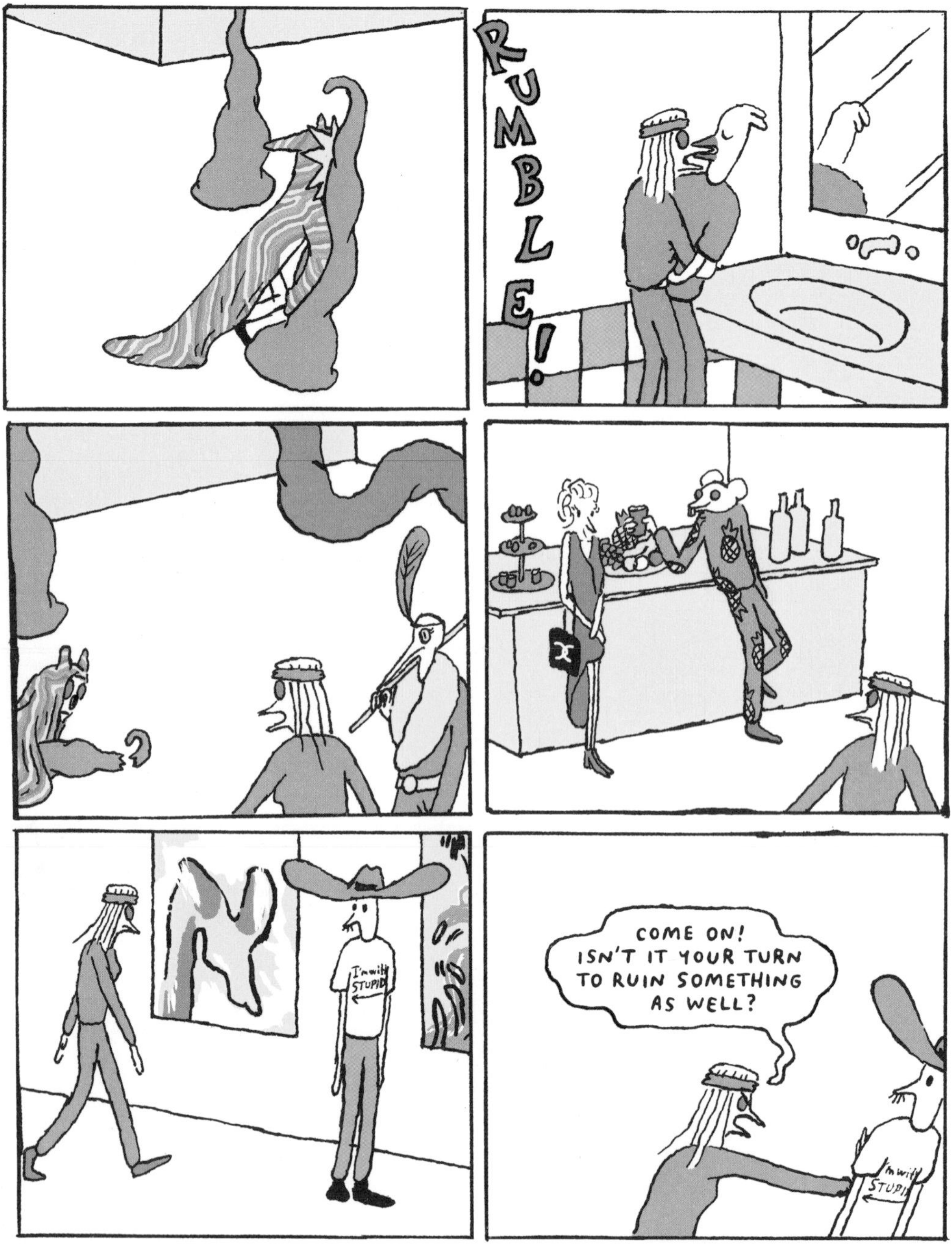
RUMBLE!
COME ON! ISN'T IT YOUR TURN TO RUIN SOMETHING AS WELL?

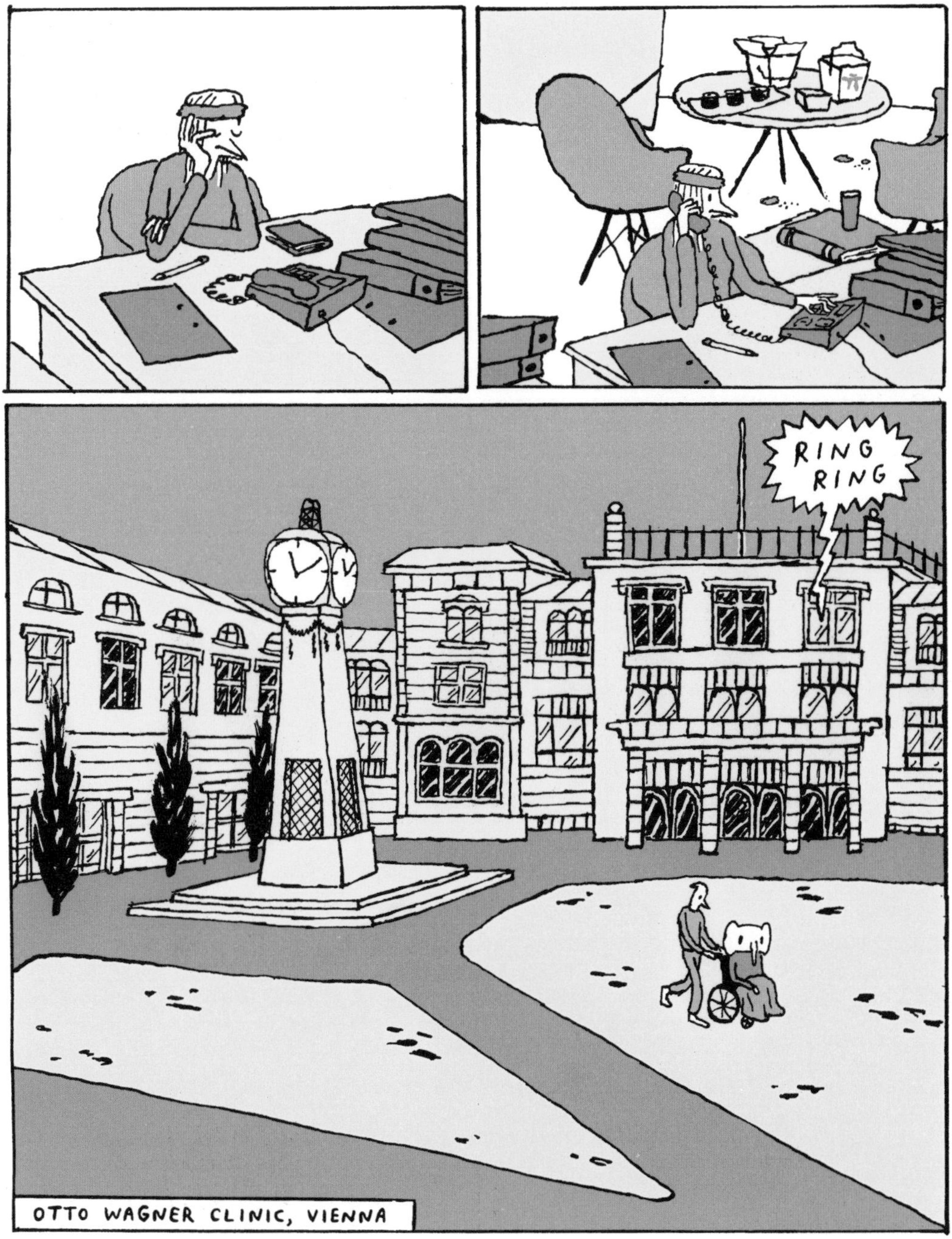
RING RING
OTTO WAGNER CLINIC, VIENNA

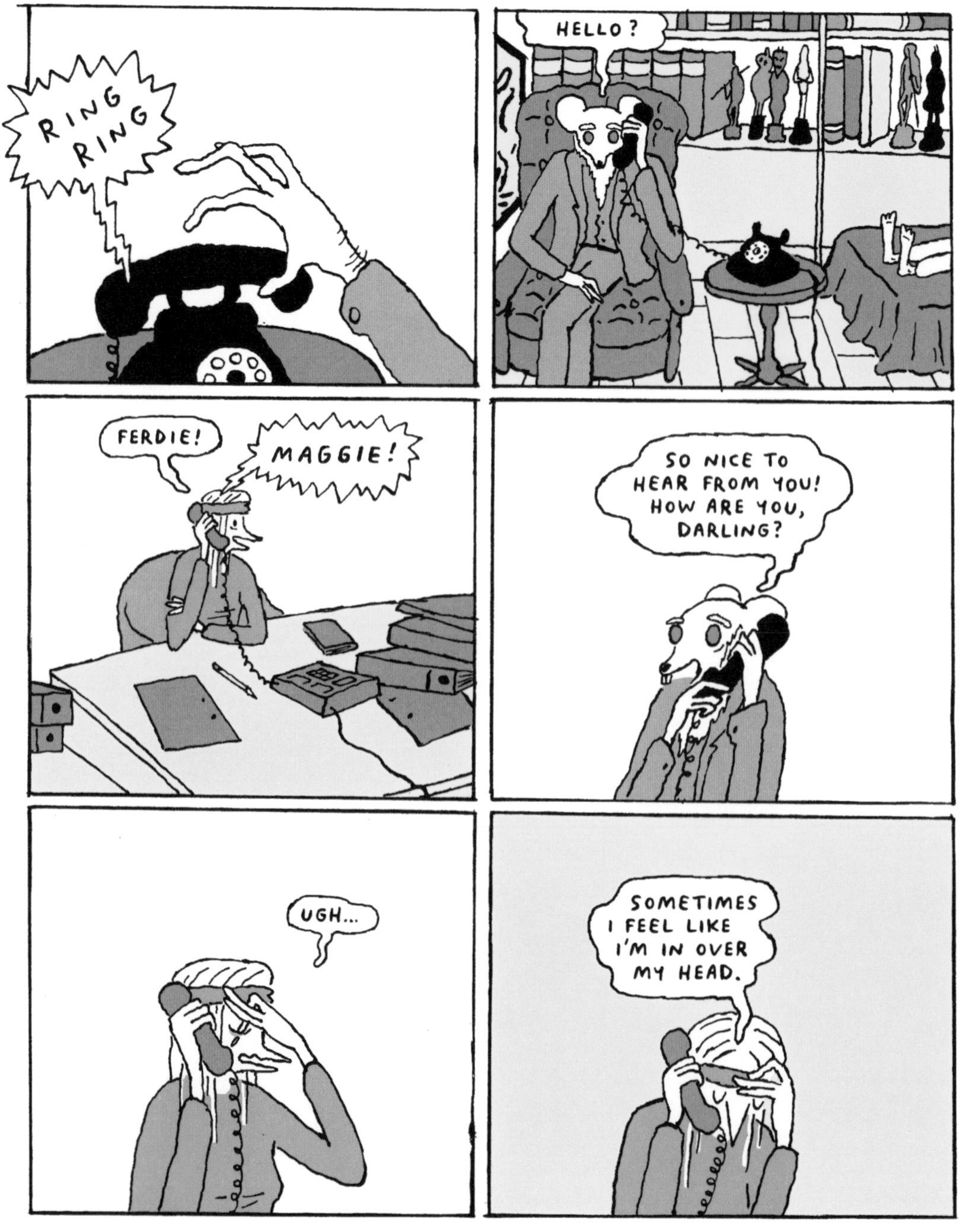
RING RING
HELLO?
FERDIE!
MAGGIE!
SO NICE TO HEAR FROM YOU! HOW ARE YOU, DARLING?
UGH...
SOMETIMES I FEEL LIKE I'M IN OVER MY HEAD.

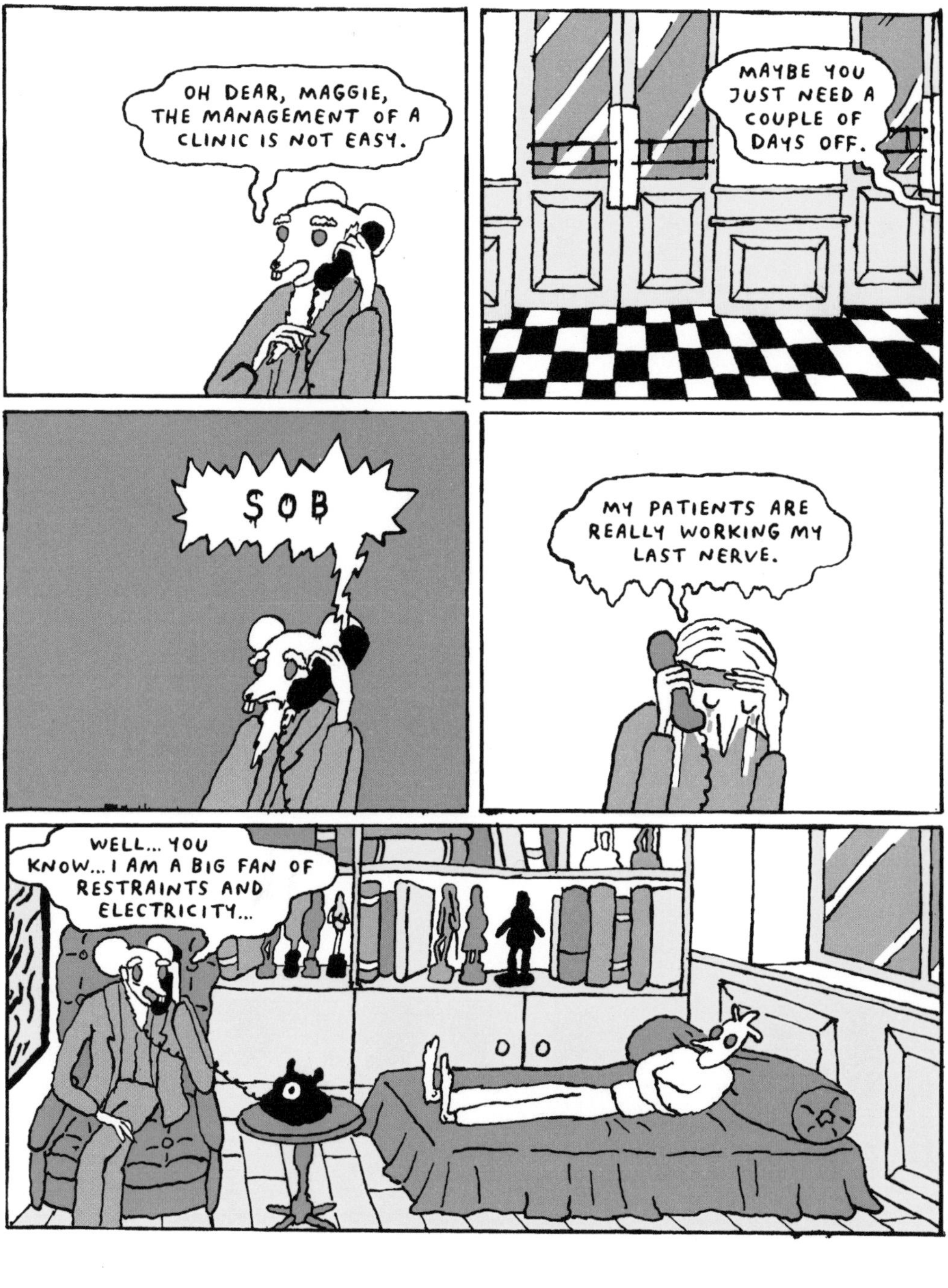
OH DEAR, MAGGIE, THE MANAGEMENT OF A CLINIC IS NOT EASY.
MAYBE YOU JUST NEED A COUPLE OF DAYS OFF.
SOB
MY PATIENTS ARE REALLY WORKING MY LAST NERVE.
WELL... YOU KNOW... I AM A BIG FAN OF RESTRAINTS AND ELECTRICITY...

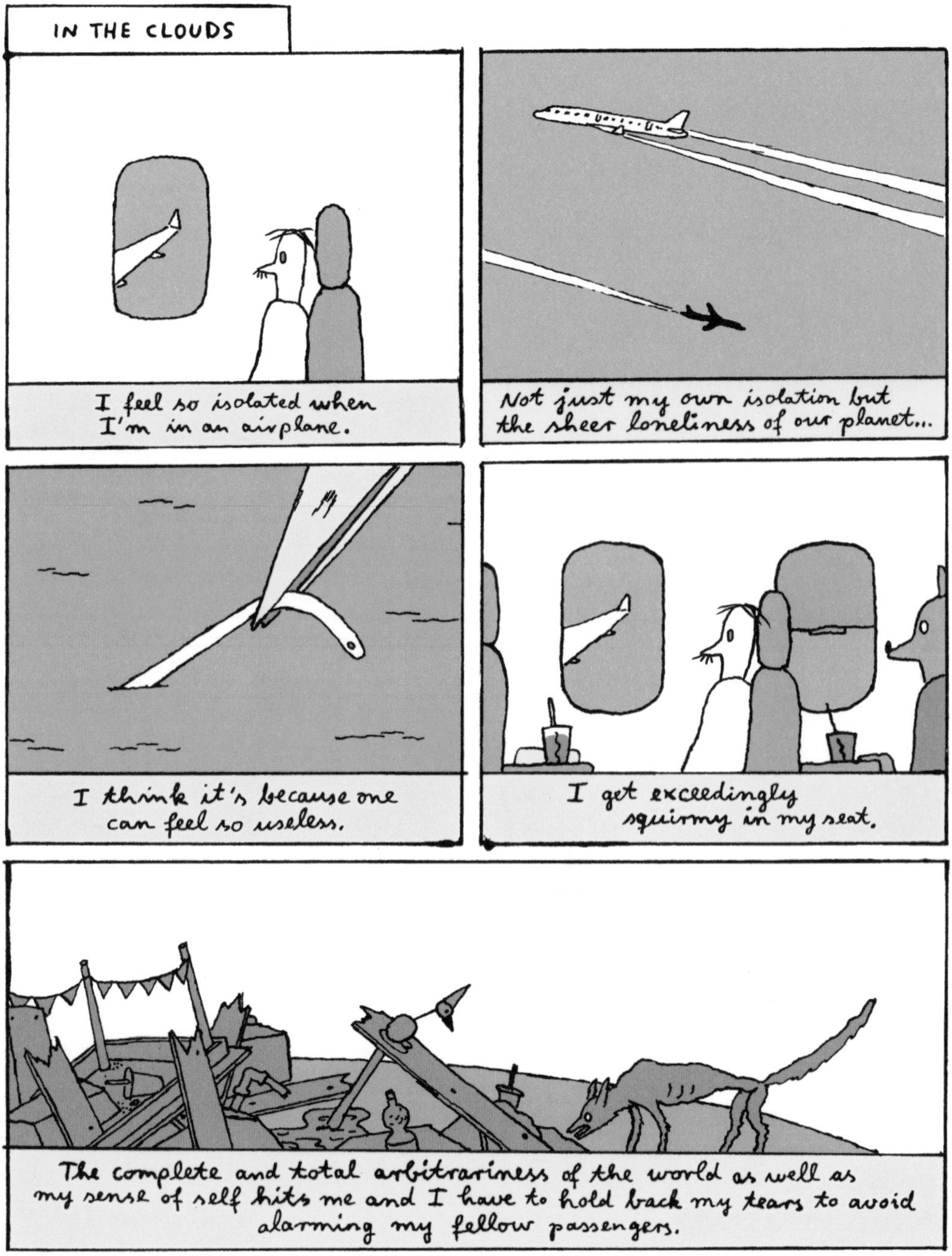
IN THE CLOUDS
I feel so isolated when I'm in an airplane.
Not just my own isolation but the sheer loneliness of our planet...
I think it's because one can feel so useless.
I get exceedingly squirmy in my seat.
The complete and total arbitrariness of the world as well as my sense of self hits me and I have to hold back my tears to avoid alarming my fellow passengers.

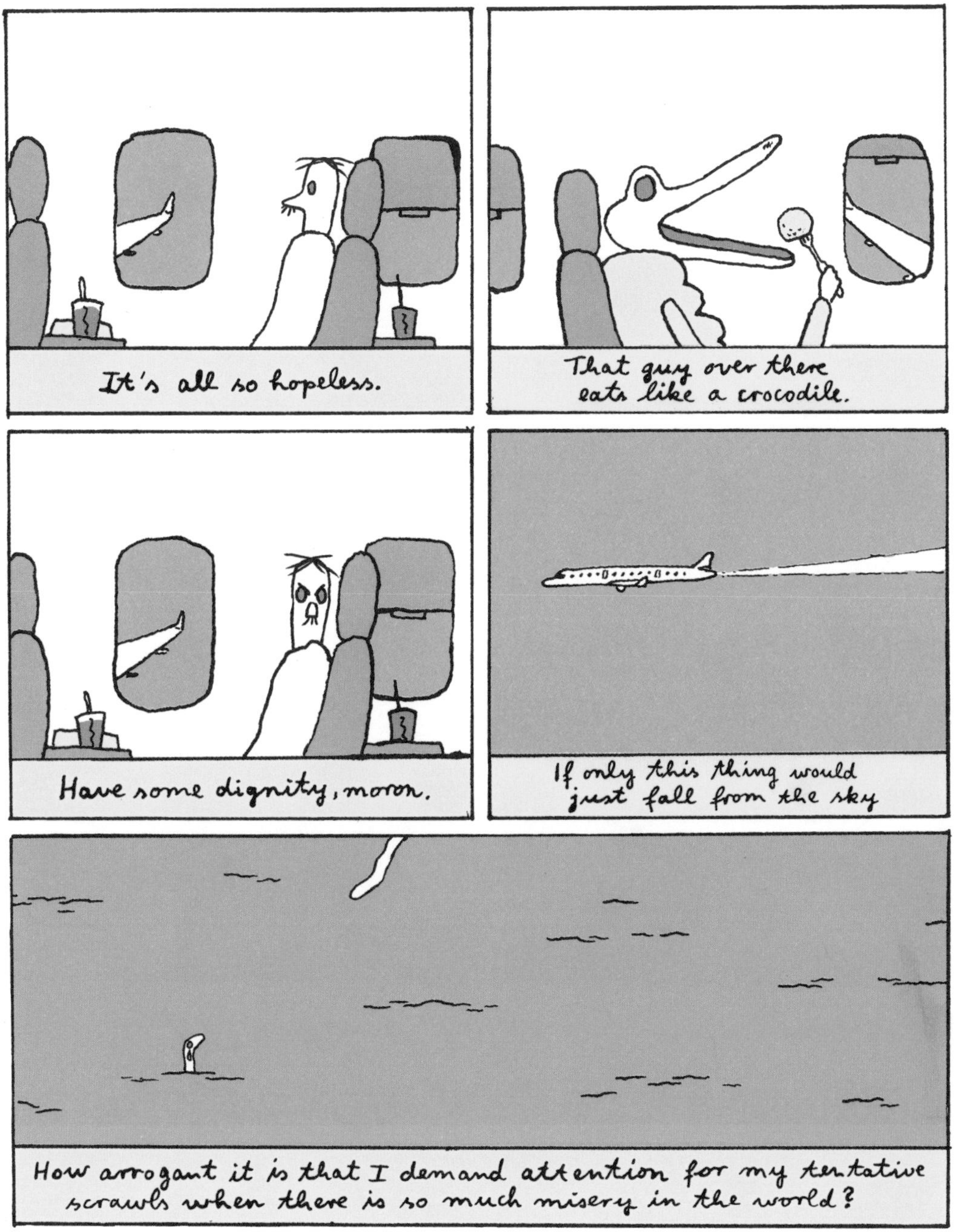
It's all so hopeless.
That guy over there eats like a crocodile.
Have some dignity, moron.
If only this thing would just fall from the sky
How arrogant it is that I demand attention for my tentative scrawls when there is so much misery in the world?

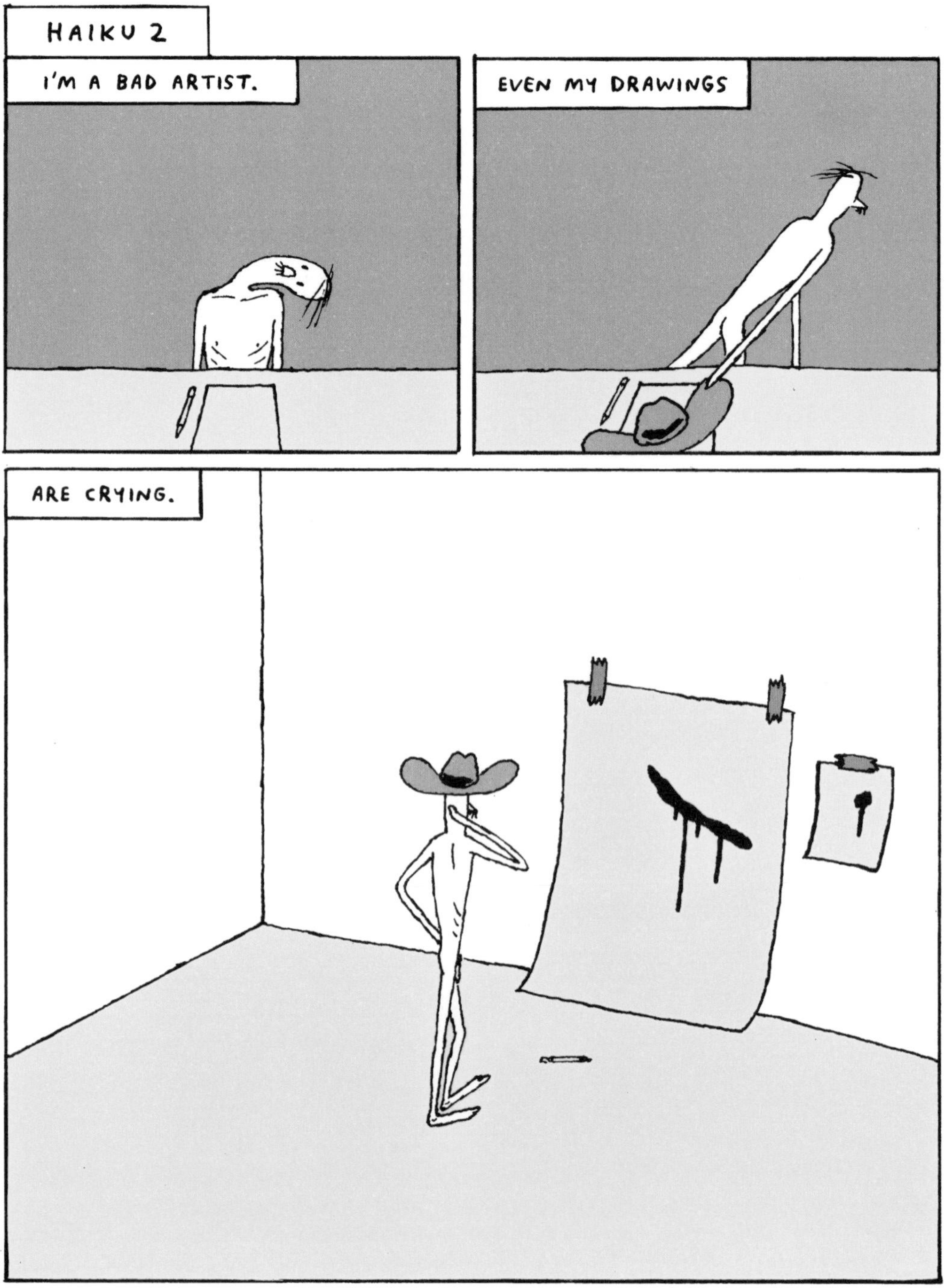
HAIKU 2
I'M A BAD ARTIST.
EVEN MY DRAWINGS
ARE CRYING.

SAUL'S CAT

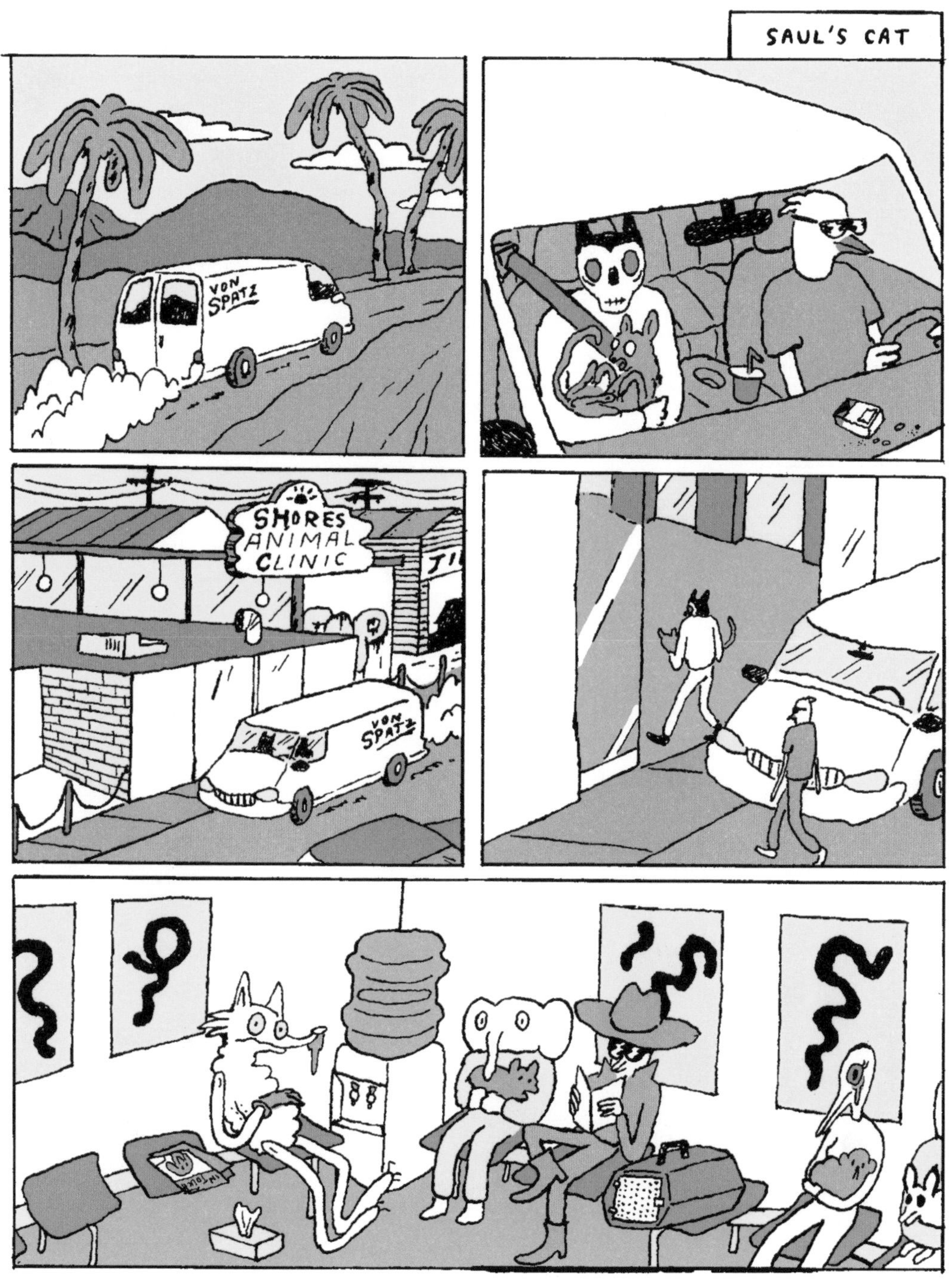
VON SPATZ
SHORES ANIMAL CLINIC
VON SPATZ

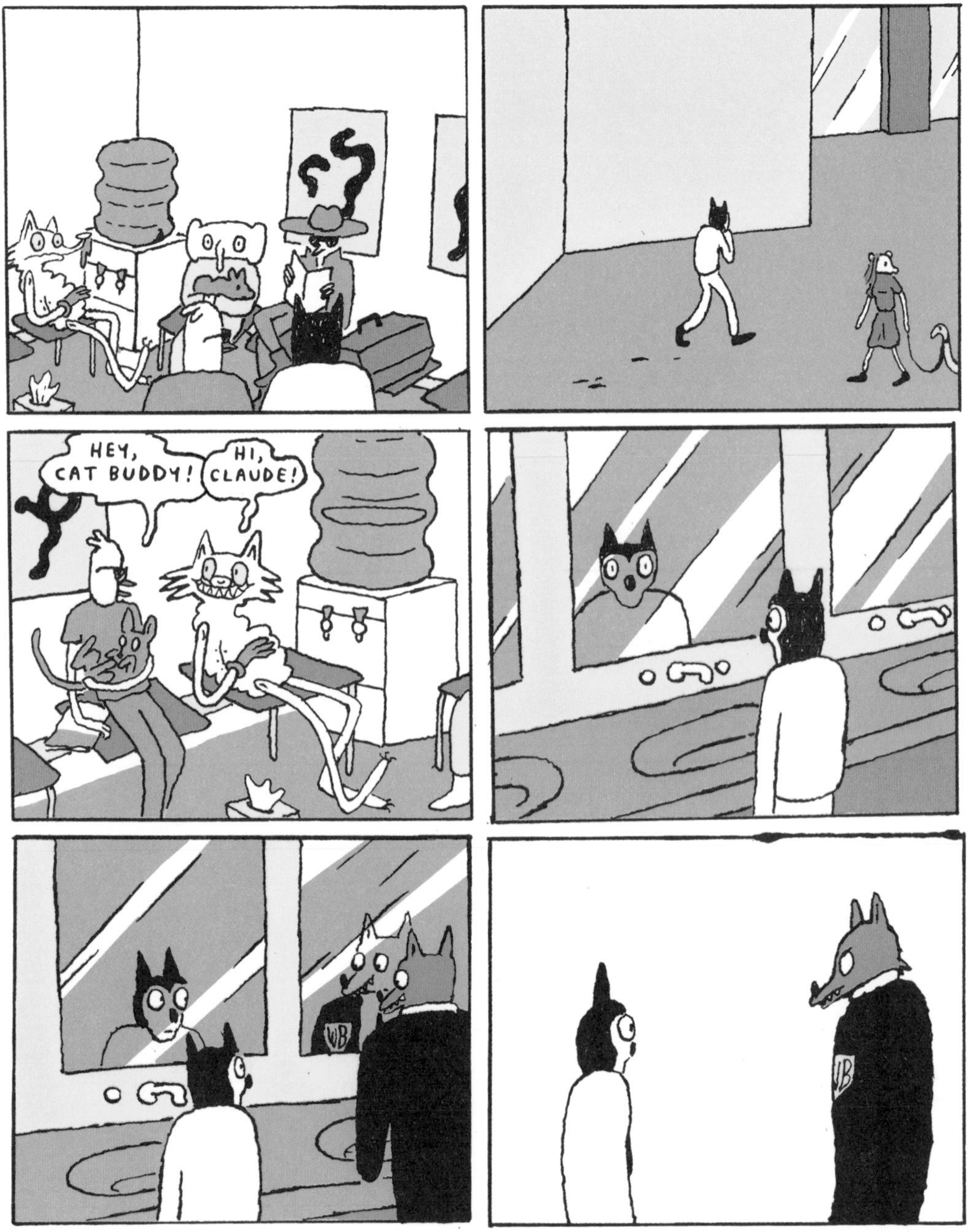
HEY, CAT BUDDY!
HI, CLAUDE!

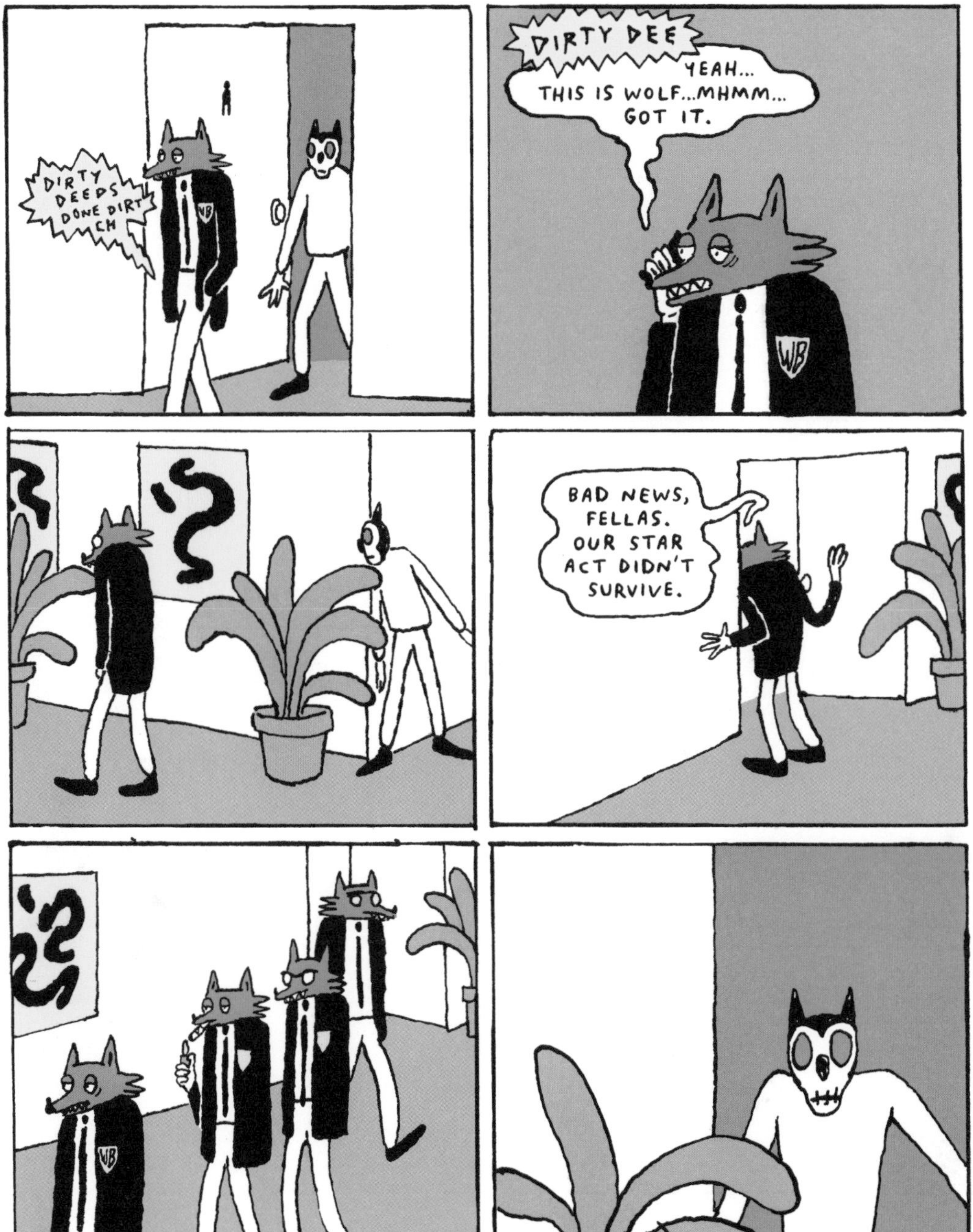
DIRTY DEEDS DONE DIRT CH
DIRTY DEE
YEAH... THIS IS WOLF...MHMM... GOT IT.
BAD NEWS, FELLAS. OUR STAR ACT DIDN'T SURVIVE.

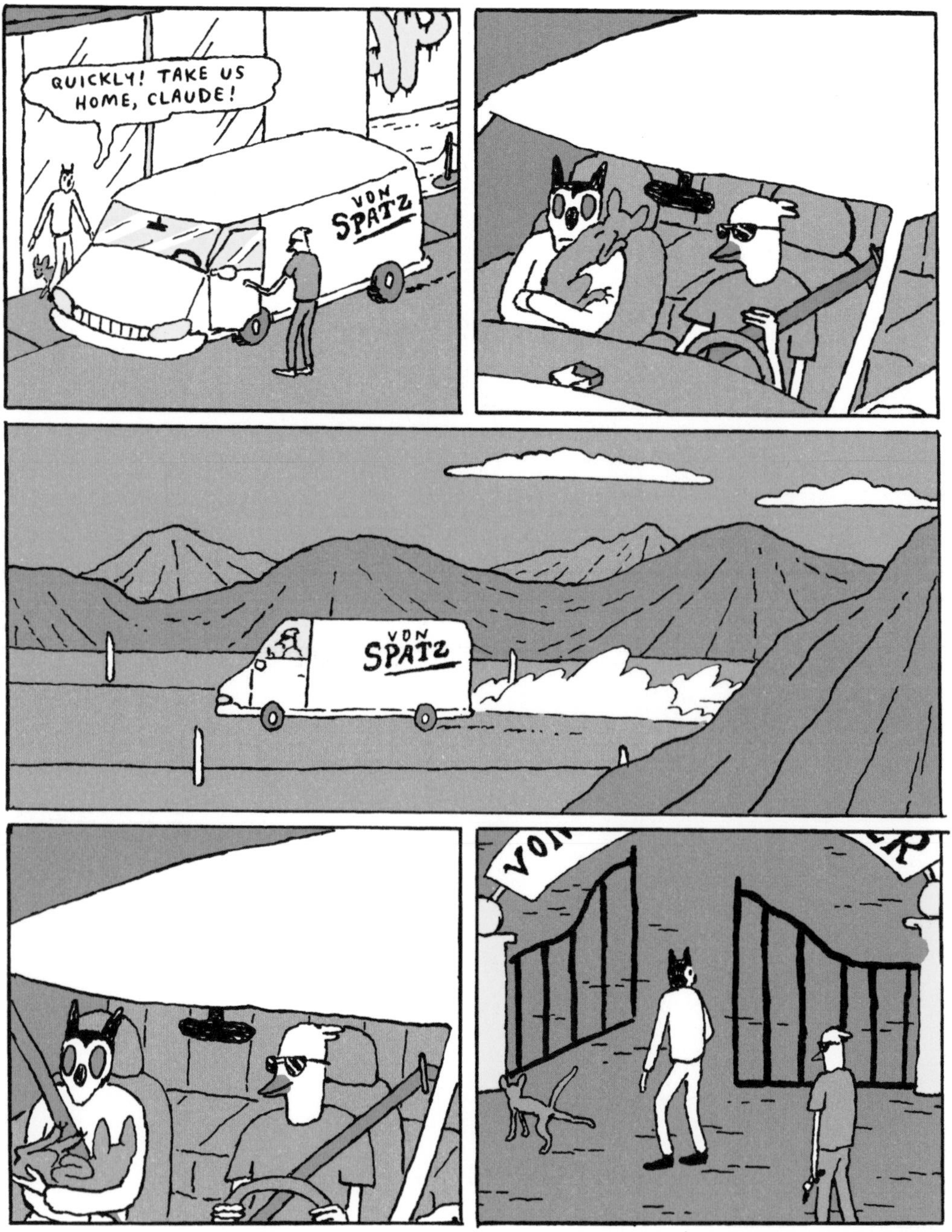
QUICKLY! TAKE US HOME, CLAUDE!
VON SPATZ
VON SPATZ

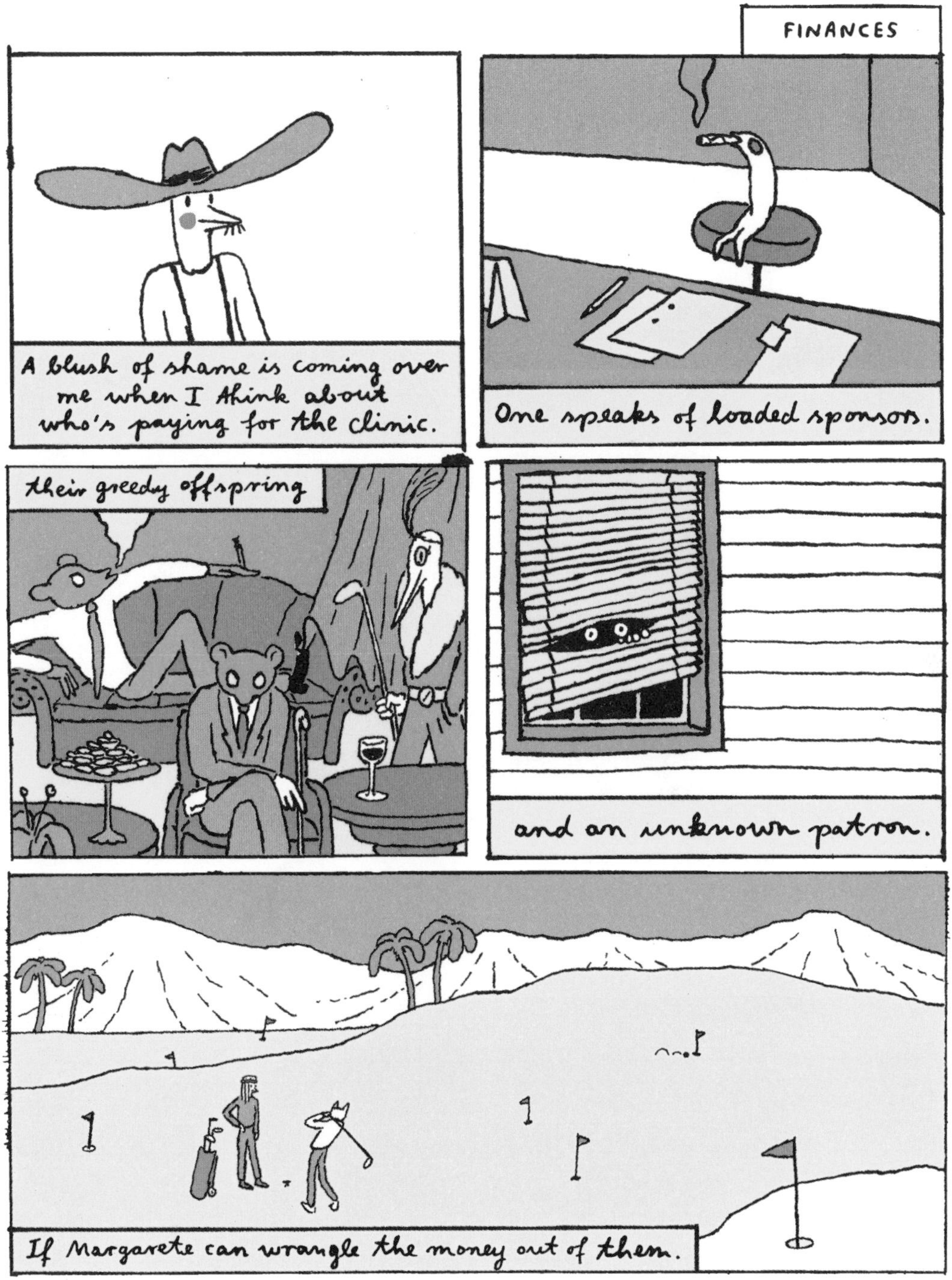
FINANCES
A blush of shame is coming over me when I think about who's paying for the clinic.
One speaks of loaded sponsors.
their greedy offspring
and an unknown patron.
If Margarete can wrangle the money out of them.

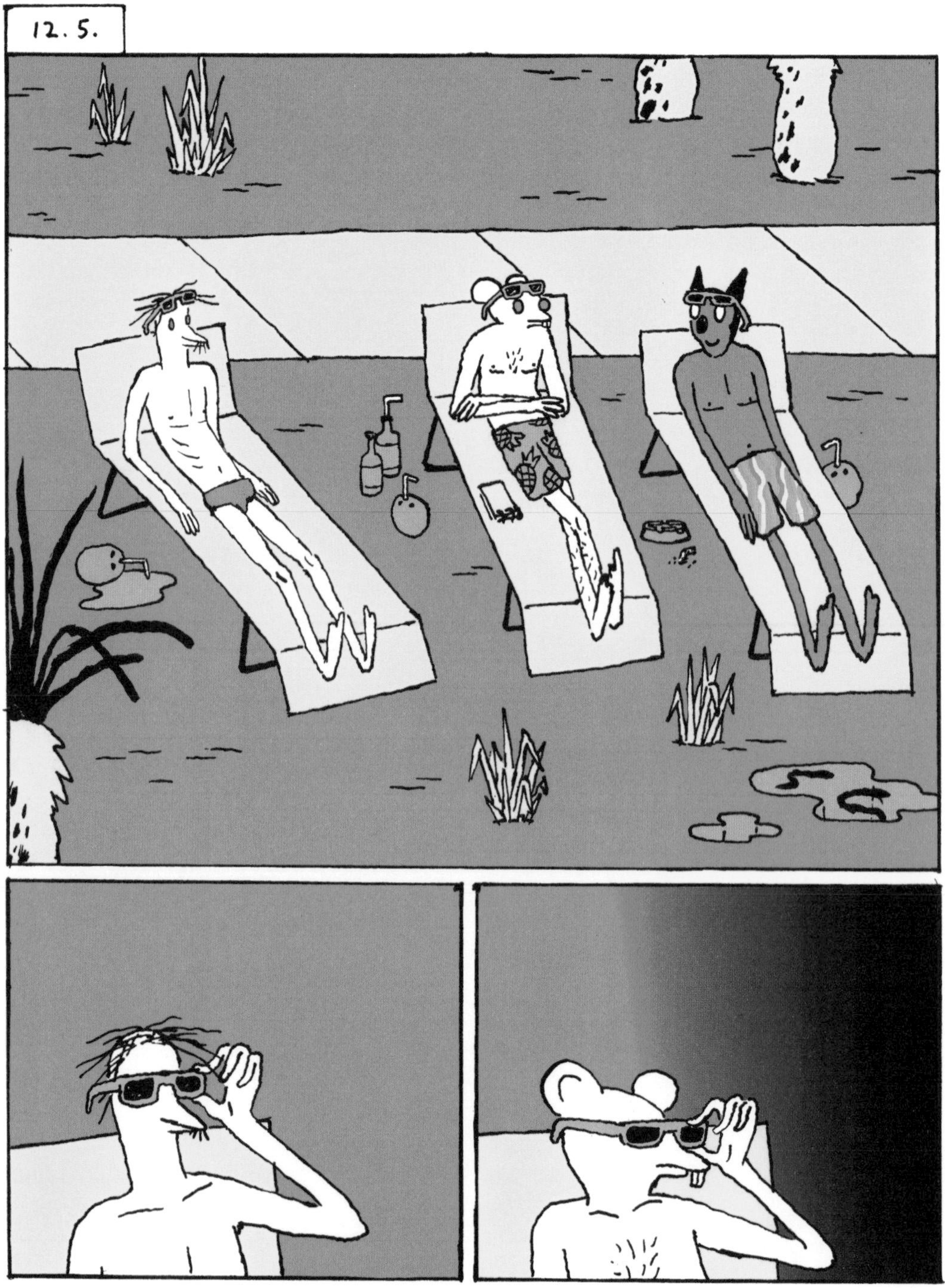
12. 5.

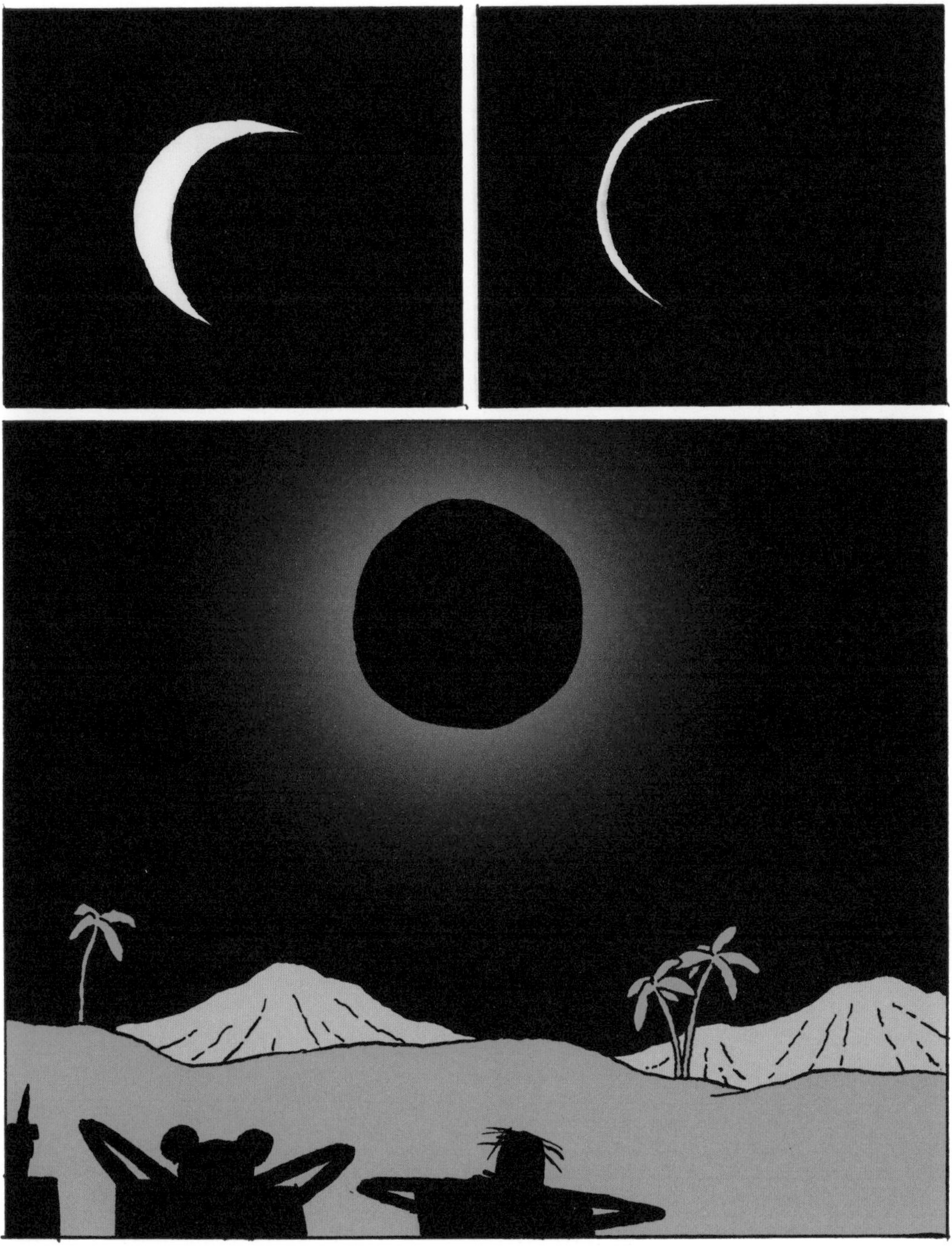

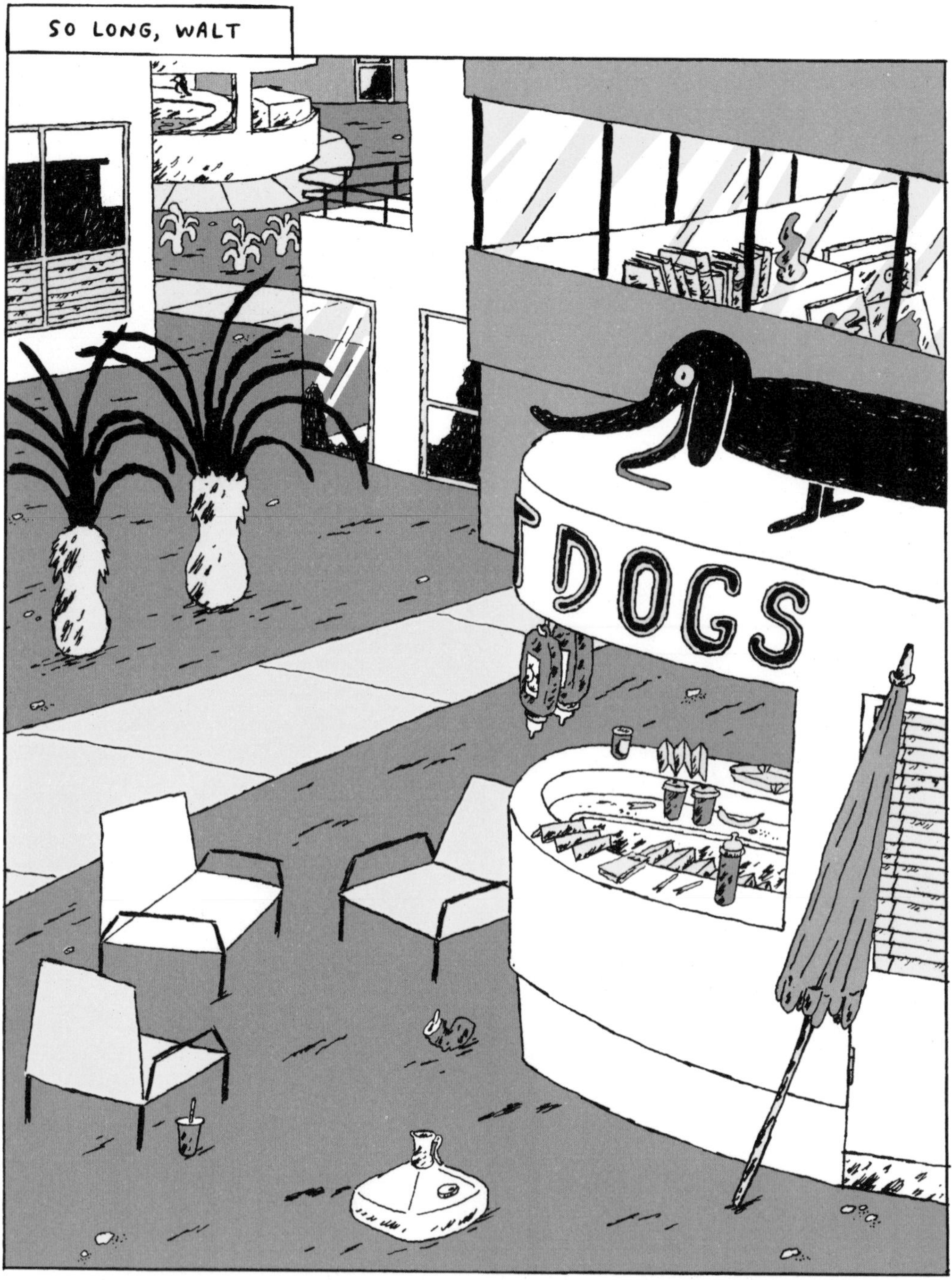
SO LONG, WALT
DOGS

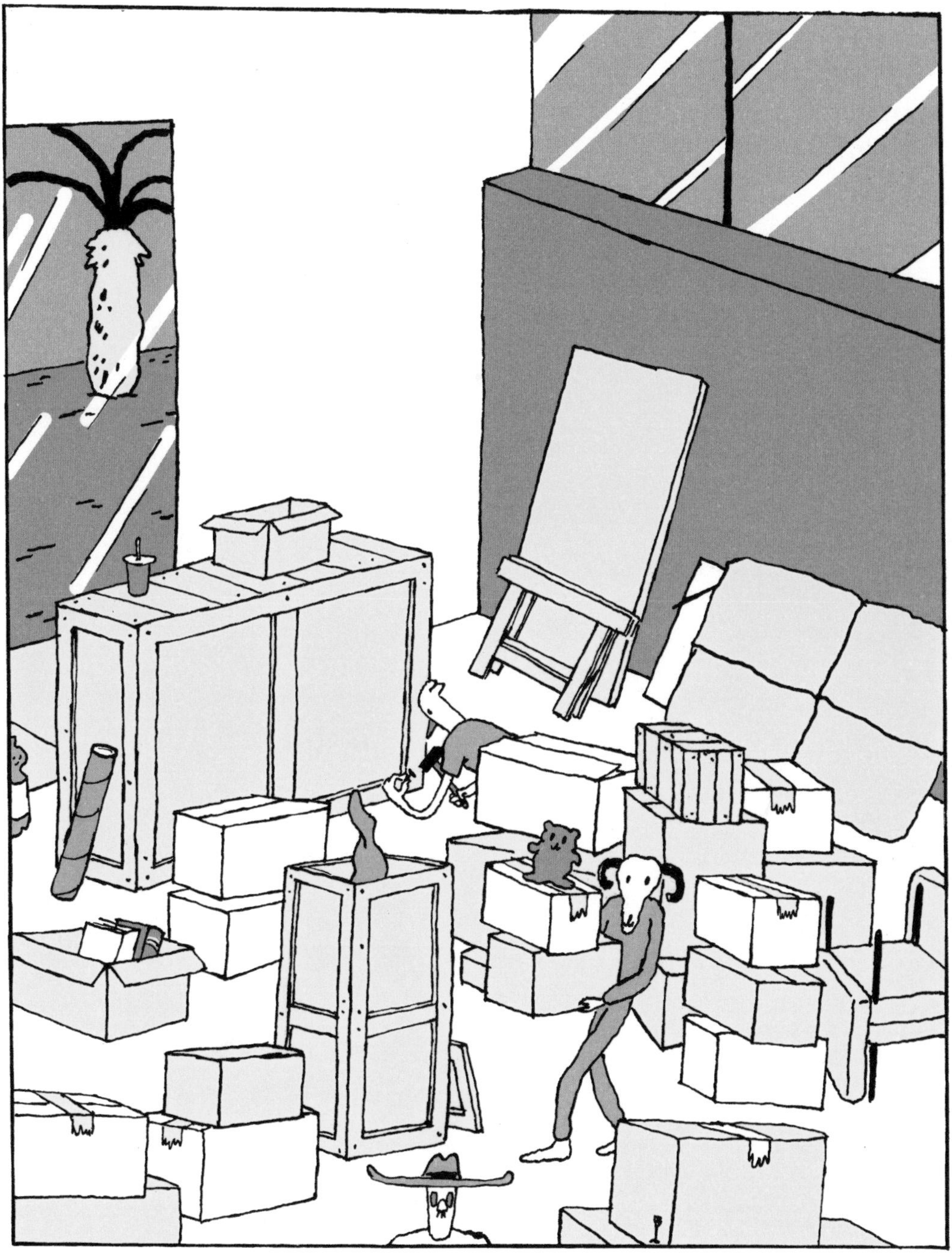

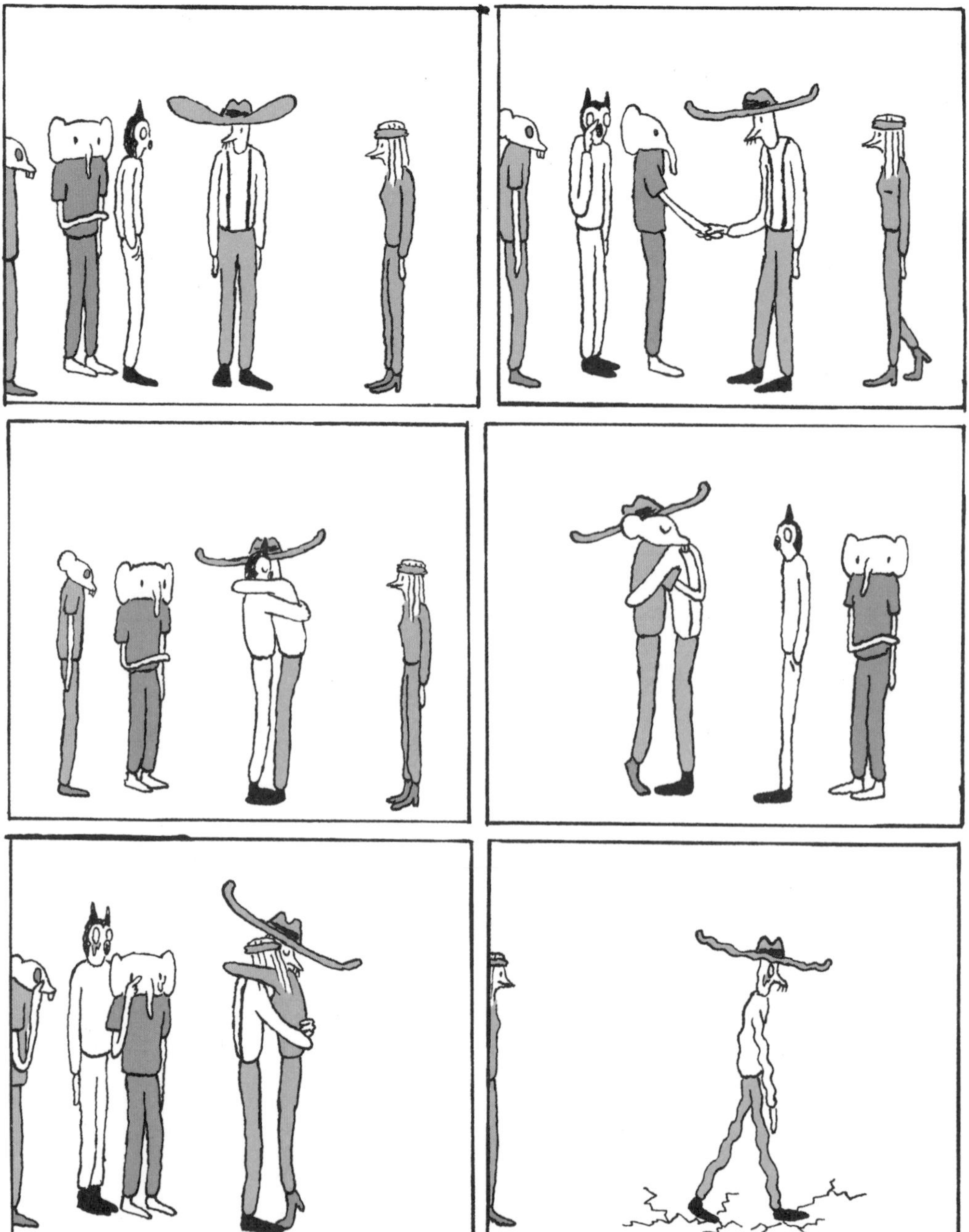

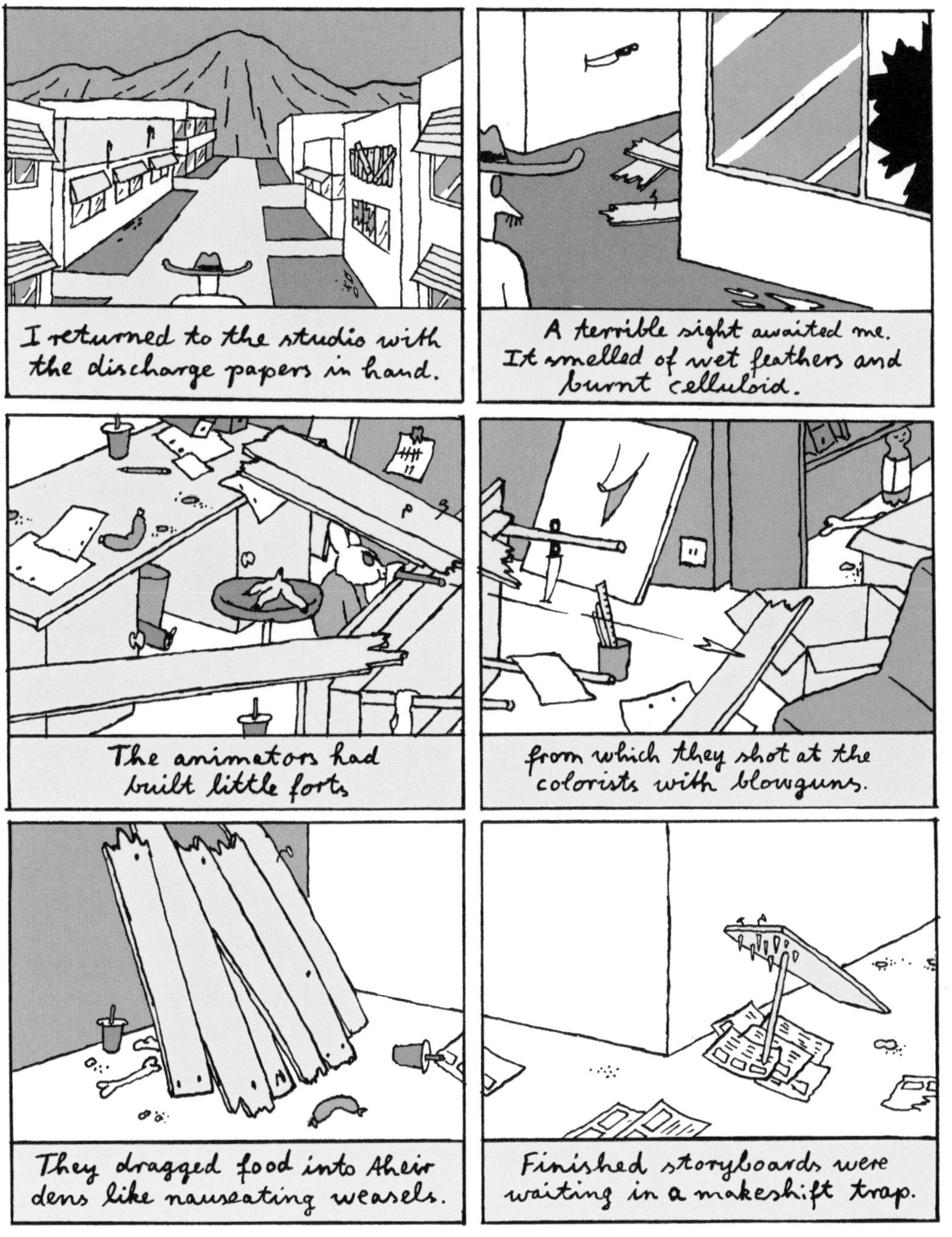
I returned to the studio with the discharge papers in hand.
A terrible sight awaited me. It smelled of wet feathers and burnt celluloid.
The animators had built little forts
from which they shot at the colorists with blowguns.
They dragged food into their dens like nauseating weasels.
Finished storyboards were waiting in a makeshift trap.

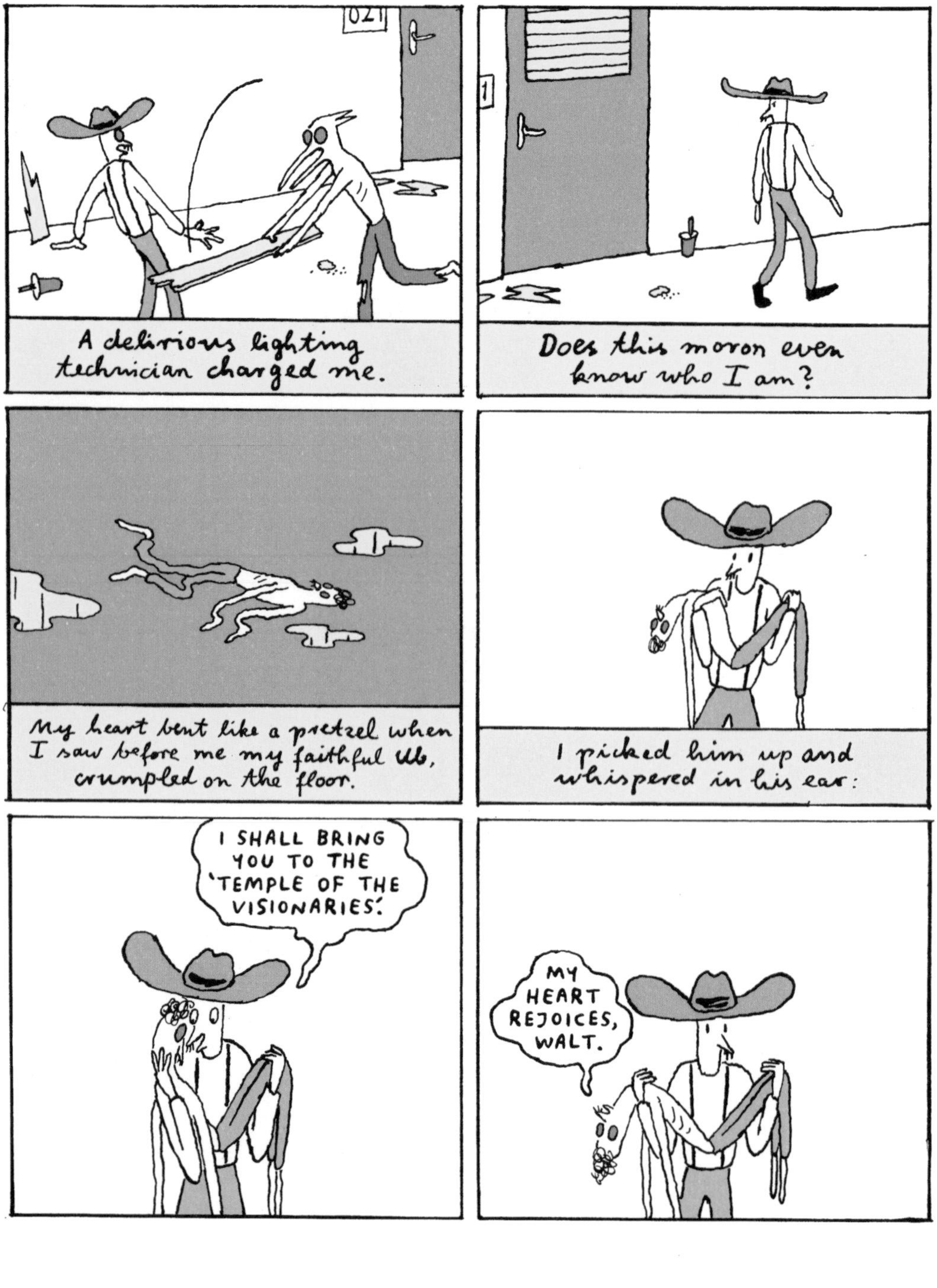

021
A delirious lighting technician charged me.
1
Does this moron even know who I am?
My heart bent like a pretzel when I saw before me my faithful Ub, crumpled on the floor.
I picked him up and whispered in his ear:
I SHALL BRING YOU TO THE 'TEMPLE OF THE VISIONARIES'.
MY HEART REJOICES, WALT.

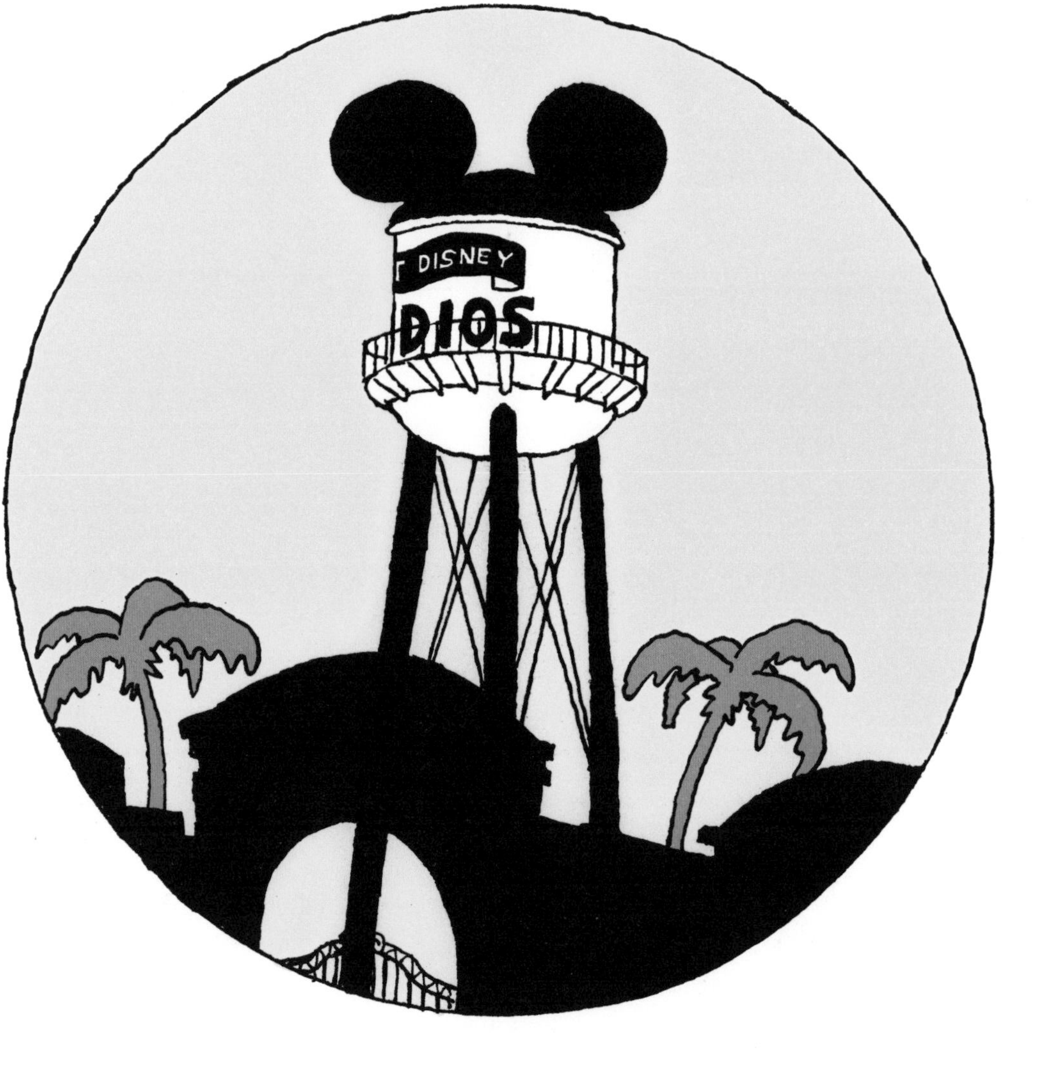
T DISNEY
DIOS

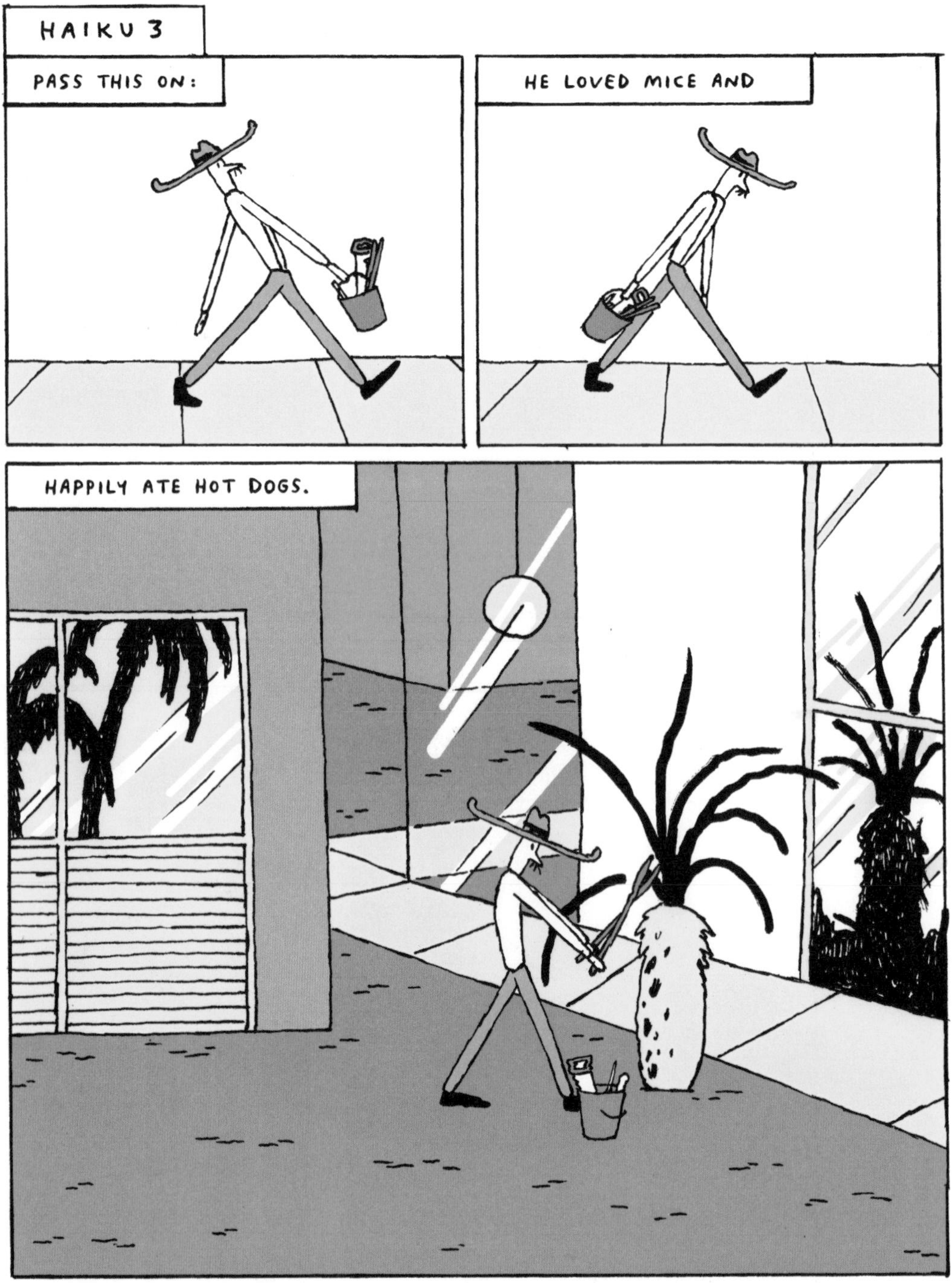
HAIKU 3
PASS THIS ON:
HE LOVED MICE AND
HAPPILY ATE HOT DOGS.